Memorizing
Made Easy

Memorizing Made Easy

Mort Herold

CONTEMPORARY
BOOKS, INC.
CHICAGO

Library of Congress Cataloging in Publication Data

Herold, Mort.
  Memorizing made easy.

  Bibliography: p.
  1. Mnemonics.   I. Title.
BF385.H43   1982   153.1'4   82-45420
ISBN 0-8092-5668-1

Published by Contemporary Books, Inc.
180 North Michigan Avenue, Chicago, Illinois 60601
Manufactured in the United States of America
Library of Congress Catalog Card Number: 82-45420
International Standard Book Number: 0-8092-5668-1

Published simultaneously in Canada by
Beaverbooks, Ltd.
150 Lesmill Road
Don Mills, Ontario M3B 2T5
Canada

To three of the best students I know,
Cress, Rich, and June

CONTENTS

PART I:
THE MEMORY CUE

1

Practical Memory Know-How

Studying has two purposes—to learn and to remember. Learning is understanding the material; but *remembering what you have learned* is what matters as far as exams and grades are concerned. Anyone who has been memorizing things by rote repetition (repeating it over and over) knows that this method is tedious, time consuming, and boring. There is a better way.

Suppose you have to memorize the terms and definitions of the following five phobias in psychology:

> acrophobia: fear of heights
> keraunophobia: fear of lightning
> ergophobia: fear of work
> iatrophobia: fear of doctors
> anthrophobia: fear of people

Right now, before reading further, look over the above terms and definitions again. Then cover up the definitions and see how many of the terms on the left you can define. Please do this now.

You'll probably agree that more time would be necessary to memorize such material. But the purpose of this book is to make memorizing of this or any other materials *considerably faster and easier*. In order for you to see how this works, let's try a simple experiment. After you read each of the following terms and definitions, carefully read and *say* each Memory Cue Sentence to the right. Make sure you notice and understand the simple associations in that sentence. Take your time. Don't rush. Do it now.

Term	Definition	Memory Cue Sentence
		(heights)
acrophobia	fear of heights.	Acrobats fear <u>high</u> jumps.
		(Keraun)
<u>keraun</u>ophobia	fear of lightning.	<u>Karen</u> is afraid of <u>lightning</u>.
		(Ergo)
<u>ergo</u>phobia	fear of work.	'Er <u>go</u> home; she no like <u>work</u>.
		(Iatro)
<u>iatro</u>phobia	fear of doctors.	I <u>atrophy</u> when I see <u>doctors</u>.
		(Anthro)
<u>anthro</u>phobia	fear of people.	<u>Aunt threw</u> the <u>people</u> out.

If you haven't actually said to yourself each of the Memory Cue Sentences, go back; read and say each one before continuing.

Now, without looking at the above, take your pencil and fill in as many of the definitions as you can.

Term	Definition
ergophobia	_____
iatrophobia	_____
keraunophobia	_____
acrophobia	_____
anthrophobia	_____

When you follow the simple directions, you see how much easier and faster these terms are to memorize and recall—if you know how to *make them easier to remember.*

This was just one quick example of the memory techniques you will learn. They are all easy, fast, and effective. The underlying principle of them all is simply to make any information you choose *easier to remember.* That's what this book is all about. It is based on one principle and one method.

- The principle: *Make it easy to remember.*
- The method: *Cue it* and *Review it!*

2

Cue It and Review It

Memory has been defined as the ability to retain and revive past impressions. When impressions are deliberately made easier to retain, they are also easier to revive. This is where the technique of *cueing your memory* comes into play.

For example, if you didn't know the word *acrophobia* at first, it was meaningless to you. But by simply using part of that word (acro), and mentally cueing it as *acrobats,* there suddenly was recognizable meaning, and your brain now had something to work with. All that remained was to come up with some thought or phrase to *connect the meaning of the term* (fear of heights) with *acrobats.* So we just used "Acrobats fear high jumps," and that was all you needed to *remind* you that acrophobia is the fear of high places.

Such memory retrieval cues are controllable, high powered, and reliable. They work. Once you set them in motion, they will not fail unless you do not set them up right in the first place. The rest of this book will teach you how to create and use memory cues properly.

You may not be aware of it, but your brain has been using a cue system all your life. When someone asks you, "What is your birthdate?'' the word *birthdate* is a cue that instantly triggers a particular month, date, and year into your mind. Actually, this information was in your head all the time, *but it took a specific cue to find and release it.*

If you hear someone merely mention the year 1492, it can instantly bring to mind Columbus discovering America. If you're walking down the street and you bump into an old friend you haven't seen for years, the mere sight of that person can flood your mind with memories of a ball game, a dance, a movie, or any other experience you both had together long ago. All of these examples involve chance encounters with various memory retrieval cues. The difference is that from now on you can use this genuinely miraculous associative power of your brain *consciously and deliberately;* you can make it work for you whenever you desire, with your study materials.

Basically, all you have to do is simply to think of another word or thought that *sounds like the original study word or thought* you want to memorize. Then you connect them into a simple memory cue sentence as we did before with the five phobias.

If you followed the directions, you should have had no difficulty in recalling all the correct definitions. One thing simply reminded you of another—and all in the blink of an eye. If you weren't able to remember all the correct definitions, you just didn't follow the directions closely enough. If this happened to you, go back to that part *now* and follow the procedure again so that you can convince yourself of the method's power.

PUTTING IT IN YOUR HEAD—
SO YOU CAN GET IT BACK OUT AGAIN

Learning is one thing, but *remembering* what you learn can be something else entirely. This is too bad, because what you are actually being graded on is not what you "know" but what you can *show* that you know. The only way you can show that you know something is to *remember it.* It may seem unfair, but if you can't remember a fact, formula, date, or concept—the practical result is the same as if you had never studied or learned it in the first place. It is for this reason that knowing not only what to know but also *how to remember what you know* is of primary importance to you in your quest for good grades and longer lasting knowledge.

The *Cue It and Review It* system is designed to enable you to learn and remember virtually any material that may be difficult for you—with far greater ease, and in a fraction of the time it takes you now.

The fact is that whenever you have trouble remembering material you learned, it's not because you have a "poor memory," but that you didn't use an appropriate memory cue technique to make it easier for your brain to remember that material. With all such material, the trick is to know how to originally *put it into your head in such a way that you can get it back out again* later. You probably didn't learn this in school. You were taught what to know, but not how to remember it. It's no different today, so it's up to you to fill in this gap. There are no poor memories, only poor learning habits.

Studies now show conclusively that the use of certain association techniques make fuller and more efficient use of the brain's natural abilities. Actually, with or without help from you, your brain is continuously making its own associative connections. But with *deliberate memory cueing,* you can supercharge your memory cells far beyond their usual performance. With this in mind, it seems obvious that by *not* using such memory aids when you need them, you can effectively hinder your power to learn and remember.

There are certain things that your brain does easiest, best, and most naturally. Among these things are the power to make associations, to form verbal and visual images, to organize, and to operate on meaning and reason. The principles of memory cueing involve these mental functions. This is how the *Cue It and Review It* system enables your memory to perform with power and efficiency.

3
___
Kinds of Memory Cues

THE SIMILAR-SOUND CUE

Memorizing the five phobias in Chapter 1 was accomplished with a specific type of memory retrieval cue which I call the *Similar-Sound Cue*. Such cues simply sound enough like the words they represent so that they instantly remind you of them. A similar-sound cue doesn't have to sound like the complete word or phrase it represents. If it sounds like only part of the word or phrase, it still works, because all you really need is a *reminder*. That's why the sound cue *Karen* reminded you of the term *keraun*ophobia. It is important for you to remember that it is the *sound*—not the spelling—that is important. Karen and keraunophobia sound enough alike so that one can remind you of the other. And, of course, the cued sentence, "Karen is afraid of lightning," gives you the meaning and definition of the term keraunophobia.

In the case of *acro*bat as a sound cue for *acro*phobia, the first part of the cue and its word are identical. The sound cue, *I atro*phy, in the cued sentence "I atrophy when I see doctors," sounds like the first three syllables in the term, *iatro*phobia. In creating your sound cues, you can use as few or as many similar sounds from the vowels and syllables of the original term as seems appropriate. Thus, the word *fortuitous* itself, could be cued as *"for two, it's us."* Fortuitous means a lucky or chance happening. Using the above similar-sound word cue, we can easily create the following cued sentence to remind us of the meaning of fortuitous:

For two, it's us—luckily!

If you are observant, you may have noticed that *fort* in fortuitious can also be cued (thought of) as fort in the word *fort*unately! This, of course, is another meaning of the term *fortuitous*. This is a built-in memory cue—a *fort*unate coincidence, and you should always be on the lookout for such ready-made cues. They make memorizing and recalling quicker and easier.

Other similar-sound cues used to learn the five phobias were:

> *'Er go* (*Ergo*phobia): sentence cued as "*'Er go* home—
>   she no like *work*." (fear of work)
> *Aunt threw* (*Anthro*phobia): sentence cued as "*Aunt
>   threw* the people out." (fear
>   of people)

Now you see how similar-sound cues work. Through similarity of sound, plus a meaningful connection with the material, they bring the original information back to mind.

THE LETTER CUE

Another type of cue is the *Letter Cue*. This is simply a word or even a non-word, each letter of which stands for a particular word. For example, the letter-cue word MIETR stands for *Make It Easy To Remember*, the basic principle of this book. Other well-known letter cues are:

ASAP: *As Soon As Possible*
ZIP: *Zone Improvement Program*
MOUSE: *Minimal Orbital Unmanned Satellite of Earth*
ERA: *Equal Rights Amendment*
NOW: *National Organization for Women*
CORE: *Congress Of Racial Equality*
UNESCO: *United Nations Educational Scientific &*
        Cultural Organization

Unlike the similar-sound cue, which actually *sounds* like the original material, the letter cue is a memory cue only because each of its letters is the same as the first letters of whatever it represents. Because of this they can be less reliable than sound cues. Sound cues practically tell you what they stand for by their sound. But if you forget what any letter in a letter cue stands for, that's the end of that! Nevertheless, letter cues have proven their usefulness and value in memorizing things. Just be sure that when you create them to help you memorize things, you pay extra attention and learn them well.

CUES AS MENTAL HOLDING DEVICES

You can think of memory cues as mental holding devices that hold information—in formation. Here are more examples, some of which may be familiar to you.

Music: Do you remember the names of the five lines of the treble clef music staff? This question itself is a memory retrieval cue that may trigger your mind to recall the letter-cue sentence, "*Every Good Boy Does Fine*," which in turn triggers the specific names of those five lines—E, G, B, D, and F. What about the four *spaces* in the music staff? You may recall them as the letter-cue word, FACE, which instantly gives you the space names—F, A, C, and E. Many such memory cues seem to be almost unforgettable once you learn them. They last for years because they create organized meaning out of something meaningless. Remember that what your brain remembers best is *meaning*.

Colors: The colors of the spectrum are Red, Orange, Yellow, Green, Blue, Indigo, and Violet. A well-known letter cue for this color sequence is the name ROY G. BIV. Another letter cue for this color sequence is *R*ich *O*ld *Y*okels *G*et *B*igger *I*n *V*igor. Still another memory cue for the color spectrum is the *sound cue, Red*'s *Or*chard is *Yellow* and *Green,* with *Blue In*sects in the *Violets.*

Geography: To memorize and recall the five great lakes (*H*uron, *O*ntario, *M*ichigan, *E*rie, and *S*uperior), just remember the letter-cue word, HOMES. To recall them in order from west to east, use this sentence: *S*ergeant *M*ajor *H*ates *E*ating *O*nions. (Or the name, S.M. HEO). The five lakes from east to west might be: *O*strich *E*ggs *H*ave *M*etal *S*hells. (Untrue, but memorable!) Lastly, a similar-sound cue wraps the five lakes up with *Eerie soup on hu*ge *Mitch.*

If you had to remember that California, Oregon, and Washington are the only three states on the west coast, you could instantly memorize this with the letter cue COW, and strengthen the verbal image with a visual image of a colossal, contented COW grazing along the entire coastline. This ties in COW with what it represents.

The only four states whose boundaries touch at the same point are Utah, Colorado, Arizona, and New Mexico. Memorize this quickly with U CAN, or CAN U, since the sequence of states is not important. If you prefer a similar-sound cue, a moment of thought might suggest something like *New Mexico*'s *aris*tocrats *collar u*tilities.

The letter cue WISE recalls that the four divisions of the British Isles are *W*ales, *I*reland, *S*cotland, and *E*ngland.

THE RHYME AS A MEMORY AID

Rhyming in order to remember is a time-tested memory

technique of considerable effectiveness. It isn't easy to forget these three classic examples:

History: In fourteen hundred ninety-two,
Columbus sailed the ocean blue.

Calendar: Thirty days hath September,
April, June, and November.
all the rest have thirty one, etc:

Spelling: i before e
except after c
or when sounded as a
as in neighbor and weigh.

OTHER KINDS OF MEMORY CUES

Seasonal Time Change: A well-known and useful reminder that millions of people recall in order to know whether to set the clock ahead or back one hour is:

Spring forward,
Fall back.

This may be the best and most generally used memory cue there is. It is brief and to the point, it reminds you *exactly,* it springs to mind whenever needed, and it seems to be unforgettable.

The Map: We've been using verbal imagery primarily in our mental cueing, but visual imagery (voluntary mental picturing) is so important that you should use it whenever you can to enhance the durability of your similar-sound or letter cueing. A prime example of the effectiveness of mental picturing is the fact that the one country on the map that everybody recognizes is Italy—because it is shaped like a boot. This visualized association usually lasts a lifetime even though it was learned many years ago in school.

Keep in mind that the purpose of these memory-cue examples is to show you how they are constructed, how they work, and to give you some idea of how effective and useful they can be to recall to mind specific material when it is needed. This relates directly to memory cueing in your academic studies. How often do you remember hearing a teacher say, "This material must be learned by Wednesday morning. I would advise you to memorize it." But are you shown *how* to memorize it? You know the answer to that one!

All knowledge is based on memory, and yet our schools and colleges have not found ways to teach the art of memory even though the techniques are now available, backed up by research, and reported in scientific journals. At the present time, this book is the only one available that is devoted entirely to *practical methods* of memorization for students. Now that you've found it, don't forget to use what you're about to learn!

4
Making the Right Connections

The law of contiguity states that any two things experienced together will become associated with each other in the mind. If you think of one thing, it will bring to mind another. This automatic reminder phenomenon is the most fundamental law of learning, and all memory cueing techniques are based on this natural law. The beauty of the law of contiguity is the ease with which it can be applied by anyone who learns how to use it. You can associate virtually any facts, ideas, words, names, dates, or concepts with one another in such a way that you can assure future recall of the material. Making the right connections is the most powerful memory activator known.

From Part II on you will learn these memory techniques through the use of practical examples as applied to a varied selection of academic subjects. Keep in mind that the basic principle throughout is simply to make the specific things you want to memorize easier to remember, and that the basic method is to *Cue it* and *Review it*.

15

You should use these techniques only when you need them —for important key points and materials that you feel may be difficult to recall in the future. It is always up to you to choose exactly which items need this high powered memory reinforcement. Once you select the exact materials, *take the time* to create good memory cues. Then all you have to do is learn them (you will find that this can happen very quickly), and then review and reinforce them as you will be taught to do.

Humor, coincidence, the unusual, and even the fanciful and illogical are all potent ingredients that activate human memory. We all remember what seems outstanding or striking to us in some way. Since these *are* the things we remember best and most naturally, we will take advantage of this engaging fact of human nature in our construction of memory cues.

If you actively participate by analyzing the cues, noting the associations involved, and occasionally memorizing and recalling the cued materials (both as directed and on your own), you will soon find that you have trained your brain to think and remember on cue.

PART II:

REMEMBERING FACTS IN VARIOUS AREAS OF KNOWLEDGE

5
History

The study of history usually involves two main things to learn and remember:

1. Identification of the event and/or date of occurrence.
2. Information: What happened, where, why, how, etc.

IDENTIFICATION

You have an upcoming exam which you feel may require you to be familiar with the drafting of the U.S. constitution in 1787. If you can remember the date without help, skip any memory aids. If you think you might forget it, here is a quick similar-sound cue that will anchor the numbers for you. First, forget about the first digit 1 in 1787. You will remember that easily enough without a cue. Just work with 787.

Step 1.

Number & Sound Cue	Number & Sound Cue	Number & Sound Cue
7 = Seven	8 = ladies	7 = heaven
(It's O.K. to use a number itself instead of a cue.)	(eighty = lady or ladies as similar-sound cues.)	(This one is a perfect rhyme.)

Step 2.

7   8   7

The number cue for 787 is: seven ladies in heaven.

Now all that remains is to come up with a simple sentence with the above number cues plus the key word, constitution.

Step 3.

Memory-Cue Sentence: A constitution was taken by seven ladies in
(cued sentence)   heaven.

Step 4.

Memorize the above short cued sentence merely by saying it over to yourself a couple of times, and you have it.

Step 5.

If the exam asks for the date of the constitution, the very word *constitution* will trigger your memorized cue sentence to mind, and all you have to do is decode "seven ladies in heaven" back into the original date (1)787. That's all there is to it. *Note:* Remember that the basic technique is not only to Cue it—but to *Review it!* In other words, in order to keep this cued sentence in mind for a few days, weeks, or months, you must review it once in a while, as you do any other study material. The cueing technique helps you to *memorize* material quickly; however, to *keep* it accessible to instant recall over a period of time, you must review it.

If the exam asks, "What happened in 1787?" the 787 will
            7   8   7
trigger: "seven ladies in heaven"—and constitution.

One thing reminds you of another.

Remember that you can create any kind of memory cue

that seems best or most appropriate to *you*. You don't have to use my cues at all. The system is flexibility itself. The beauty of it is that anything you create yourself you will remember best, *because* it took increased attention and concentration on your part, and thus a much deeper original impression was made.

INFORMATION ABOUT THE EVENT

Suppose that you must know the following three basic points established in the 1787 constitution:

1. The constitution established a balance of power between the federal and state governments.

2. It established a bicameral legislature (the house and senate) rather than a parliament.

3. It provided for legislators and a chief executive to be elected for limited terms.

As always, *you must first study and understand the information itself.* Then you select key words to remind you of specific key points, and arrange them in whatever sequence is best for memorization. These selected key words are your memory cues which you now string into some kind of appropriate sentence that is easy to remember. Let's say that you select the following points and initially cue them like this:

(From basic point #1:) Balance of power between federal and state governments. All you need here is the cue word *balance.* If you have studied the material, the cue, *balance,* will remind you of the details easily enough.

(From basic point #2:) Bicameral legislature rather than a parliament. *Bicameral* is the only cue you need to trigger the rest. But "bicameral" may seem a little too abstract for a cue, so why not use the similar-sound cue, *buy cameras,* instead. You'll see how this will work in a moment.

(From basic point #3:) Legislators and chief executive to be elected for limited terms. Let's use the cue words, *chief* and *limited legislators.* (By your understanding of point 3, you'll know that *both* the chief executive and the legislator are elected for limited times.)

In this way, using these sound cues (some of which are the original words in this case) you can come up with a cued sentence somewhat as follows:

			(chief
	(balance		executive,
	of		limited
	power)	(bicameral)	term)
The Constitution	balances	and buys cameras	chiefly for

(legislators
elected for
limited terms)
limited legislators.

As before, you now repeat this sentence to yourself a few times until you have it down pat without looking at it. Again, by decoding each cue as you think of the sentence, you will have no trouble at all in recalling the complete information. Right now, study the original three basic points first listed, and then commit the above cued sentence to memory. Then see for yourself how efficiently you can reconstruct and recall the three points about the 1787 constitution.

It is, of course, important to take the time to think up a good cued sentence. You may come up with two or three at first. Just select one that you think fits your purposes best, and then learn it. You'll be saving much time in the long run, besides ensuring far more reliable recall when it counts. As with any other worthwhile technique, practice develops speed. You will also find that this kind of study-memorization is far more enjoyable and rewarding than constant re-reading or tiresome rote repetition.

THE STORY CUE

A logical extension of similar-sound sentence cueing is the

story cue. If the material you choose to memorize is lengthy and more detailed, you can use a *succession of cued sentences* to hold the key points in mind. In other words, you make a *story* out of it. Gordon Bower, a leading memory authority at Stanford University, has done extensive research with such a method; he calls it "narrative chaining." Students using this method learn and remember far more material in much less time than students who use the usual methods of study and memorization.

Following is a practical example of the story cue in action (showing how what seem to be difficult abstractions can be efficiently memorized with this approach). In order to pass anatomy, medical students must learn and remember the following list of the twelve cranial nerves.

olfactory	facial
optic	acoustic
occulometer	glossopharyngeal
trochlear	vagus
trigeminal	spinal accessory
abducens	hypoglossal

We will now cue these words as reminders, and string them into a little "story" made up of only two cued sentences. This is a condensed version of Gordon Bower's narrative chain of this material.

The *oil factory*'s (olfactory) *optician* (optic) *occupied* (occulometer) a *truck* (trochlear) in which *three gems* (trigeminal) were *abducted* (abducens) by a *face* (facial) with *ears* (acoustic). A *glossy photograph* (glossopharyngeal) of them was *vague* (vagus) and appeared *spineless* (spinal accessory) and *hypocritical* (hypoglossal).

Here is the two-sentence story by itself:

The *oil factory*'s *optician occupied* a *truck* in which *three gems* were *abducted* by a *face* with *ears*. A *glossy photograph* of them was *vague* and appeared *spineless* and *hypocritical.*

In this way, ordinarily difficult-to-memorize material is simplified, and learned as only two sentence units, rather than 12 individual technical terms to be digested by brute repetition!

In Chapter 15 you will learn an advanced memory cue system in the form of a mental file rather than a story. The mental file accommodates lengthy and voluminous materials for memorization and includes this story cue method when needed. It's a good idea for you to be familiar with *story cueing* at this point, both for immediate use and in preparation for the advanced cueing section of this book. But right now let's get back to the subject of history.

MORE HISTORICAL EVENTS AND HOW THEY CAN BE CUED FOR EASIER MEMORIZATION

Event and Date	Memory Retrieval Cues
The Boston Tea Party, 1773.	17 Boston Tea Party tosses out seventeen tons 73 of heavenly tea.
Philadelphia founded, 1682.	16 8 Philadelphia found a sweet sixteen lass who ate 2 two cream cheeses.
Salem Witchcraft Trials, 1692.	6 Salem Witchcraft Trials fix 92 witches.
Washington inaugurated as first president, 1789.	8 Washington was inaugurated at age 17, and ate 9 fine!

Such cued sentences should not, of course, be taken literally.

If you're good at rhyming, why waste your talent? You can use it to compose a *rhyme cue* or two:

> In seventeen hundred eighty-nine,
> Washington was *first* in line.

This may not establish you as a published poet, but you *will* remember the material. Simple two or four line rhymes are easy to think up, and they have a tendency to stick tenaciously. Remember the one about Columbus sailing the ocean blue?

Event and Date	*Memory Retrieval Cues*
	0 4
Napoleon proclaimed Emperor, 1804.	Napoleon, at 18, opted for emperor.
	8 (St.
Death of Napoleon on St. Helena, 1821.	Napoleon's fate was a 21 gun salute as a Saint Helena) in hell.

Napoleon's birth and death dates in rhyme cues:

> Napoleon was born to boo
> In seventeen hundred thirty-two
> When heaven called, his work was done
> In eighteen hundred twenty-one.

` Many times you will already remember in which century an event occurred. In such cases, all you need to cue are the last two numbers instead of all four. Here are a few examples:

Event and Date	Memory Retrieval Cues
Lincoln-Douglas Debates, 1858.	<div align="center">5 8</div>Lincoln-Douglas debates will be live at eight!<div align="center">(or)</div><div align="center">5 8</div>Lincoln-Douglas live de-bate.
Lincoln inaugurated president, 1861.	At inauguration, Lincoln was 6 foot 1.
Lincoln assassinated, 1865.	When Lincoln was assassinated, he weighed 65 pounds. (Not true—but what a cue! If it were true, who could forget it?)

If you wanted to memorize all three of the above Lincoln events, you could make one long cue sentence, or two shorter ones. Or, you might prefer these easy-to-remember rhyme cues:

> Lincoln debate—in fifty-eight
> Lincoln's the one—in sixty-one
> Lincoln alive—in sixty-five?
> No.

Event and Date	Memory Retrieval Cues
U.S.-Mexican War, 1846.	The U.S.-Mexican War lasted only 46 minutes.
Pasteur develops innoculation against hydrophobia, 1885.	<div align="left">8 5</div>Pasteur ate five germs and developed hydrophobia.
The Civil War, 1861 to 1865.	The Civil War was shooting live (sixty-one) But Dixie's done in sixty-five.

Event and Date	*Memory Retrieval Cues*
Ratification of amendment permitting income tax, 1913.	"'13 was a bad luck year. Income tax started."

17

| U.S. declares war on Germany, 1917. | U.S. declares war on seven teens in Germany. |

20

| Birth of the League of Nations, 1920. | One League of Nations was plenty.
(or)
Twenty Thousand Leagues Under the Sea
(A famous novel by Jules Verne) |

(twenty-seven)

| Lindbergh flies the Atlantic, 1927. | Lindbergh flew the sunny heavens over the Atlantic.
(or)
Lindy was in seventh heaven
When he flew in twenty-seven. |

2   9

| The Stock Market Crash, 1929. | The Stock Market crashed to-night. |

3   5

| The Social Security Act, 1935. | Social Security—be live and cautious. |

'4   1

| U.S. declares war on Japan, 1941. | For one act, we declared war on Japan. (Pearl Harbor, 12/7/41) |

| 1945:
Roosevelt dies;
Truman becomes president;
first atomic bomb,
on Hiroshima. | (Three events in one year, cued in rhyme:)
Roosevelt died in forty-five
But Harry Truman did arrive.
First atomic bomb will dive
But Hiroshima won't survive. |

Event and Date	Memory Retrieval Cues
	(Alaska) (Hawaii)
Alaska and Hawaii admitted as states, 1959.	Q: <u>I'll ask 'ya—how-ah-ya?</u> (fifty - nine) A: <u>Nifty - fine!</u>
Kennedy assassination, 1963.	Sad to see . . . <u>Kennedy</u> Catastrophe <u>Sixty-three.</u>

                                                 (Armstrong)

Neil Armstrong walks on moon, 1969.	<u>6</u> foot <u>9</u> <u>moon</u>-man with <u>strong arms.</u>

                               7   2

Watergate scandal, 1972.	<u>Watergate—seven boos!</u>
Nixon term and resignation, 1968–1974.	<u>Nixon's</u> presidential date Began in nineteen <u>sixty-eight</u> But <u>resignation</u> loomed in store He flew the coop in <u>seventy-four.</u>

With few exceptions it usually isn't necessary for you to remember complete and exact dates in history—with month, date, and year. But for the sake of completeness (and the possibility of future necessity) the following is an easy method, based on what you've learned so far, to take care of this contingency.

Here are a few historical figures of the future, with complete birthdates in single sentence cues:

Individual and Birthdate	Memory Retrieval Cues
	12 / 1/ 3 5
Woody Allen 12/1/35	<u>Woody Allen</u> told a <u>dozen</u> and <u>one dirty lies.</u>

Individual and Birthdate	*Memory Retrieval Cues*
Arthur Rubinstein 1/28/87	1/ 28/ Rubinstein has 1 piano, 28 inches high, with 87 87 keys.
Orson Welles 3/6/15	3/ 6/ 15 Orson Welles does three tricks in fifteen minutes.
Luciano Pavarotti 10/12/35	10/12/ 3 5 Pavarotti sings as ten dozen birdies fly.

6

Numbers and Mathematics

THE HEROLD NUMBER MEANING METHOD

Numbers

Memory blanks for all kinds of numbers is an old story. Aside from remembering names, the one thing that many people seem to have trouble with is remembering (or memorizing) numbers. The basic reason for this is that numbers in themselves have little meaning. On the other hand, *words,* in themselves, do have meaning, and are consequently much easier to remember. If you wanted to memorize and recall the following sentence, you would have very little trouble:

Einstein had a bagel, cheese, and coffee for breakfast.

Now look at the following number just *once,* and then try to recall and repeat it as you look away:

1418210311492

As you can see, it is not always easy to remember numbers. But if you could give those same numbers some definite *meaning,* the story might be different.

If you cue the previous numbers as:

1 = I (letter I is a "look-alike" cue)
4 = for (similar-sound cue)
1 = one   "   "   "
8 = ate   "   "   "
2 = too   "   "   "
1031 = 10/31 (October 31, *Halloween*—a date symbol cue)
1492 = Columbus (a name symbol cue)

then you can cue this into a sentence such as:

1 4 1 8 2   10/31   1492
I, for one, ate too—on Halloween, with Columbus.

You have now transformed meaningless numbers into a sentence with meaning. Now all you have to do is simply memorize that *sentence* (not the numbers!). To recall the numbers easily to mind, you merely repeat the sentence to yourself, and mentally decode each of the cue words back into the original numbers. Of course, this is exactly what you were doing with shorter numbers (dates) in Chapter 5 (History).

The system is simplicity itself. You cue it and review it. By following this procedure for specific numbers that you feel you may forget (and which may be important) you will greatly shorten memorization time, and greatly increase your reliability of recall.

In Chapter 5, we used mostly similar-sound cues. Symbol cues (1031 = Halloween; 1492 = Columbus) are also easy to use. Whatever number can represent or symbolize a particular date, event, person, or fact is a symbol cue. Be on the lookout for such cues, because numbers are *full of them.* They are "built-in" memory aids, and when you use them in conjunction with similar-sound cues, number memorization becomes a comparative snap.

Try to use two, three, four, or more digits at a time to create a single cue whenever you can. This way, you can shorten the number of words in your cued sentence. The shorter your sentence cues, the easier and longer you can remember them.

Following is a list of some similar-sound cues and symbol cues for various numbers. It is not complete (that would take a book in itself), but it will help you to create your number memory cues while you're still a beginner with this system. Use it for reference when you can't think of a suitable word or meaning for a number. Remember that similar-sound cues needn't be exactly similar in sound to the original word. All you need is a *reminder. Any* word or phrase that will remind you effectively can do the job. Even vowel sounds alone can be efficient reminders for numbers.

For example:

5 = fly, by, high, as well as hive, drive, chives, arrive. (With number 9, the vowel sound i in nine sounds the same as the i in five. Be careful; don't confuse these two. For number 9 cues, use either an exact rhyme or a cue word starting with n for nine.)

9 = wine, pine, (plurals OK, as pines), dine, or night, nice, etc.

0 = Oh, bow, mow, dough, or (if you like) any word starting with letter O, or Z (for Zero.)

SAMPLE LISTING OF SIMILAR-SOUND CUES AND SYMBOL CUES FOR NUMBERS

0. *Similar-Sound Cues:* Oh, dough, ogle, opal, Joe, Flo, open, owl, zoo, zip.
   Symbol Cues: circle, wheel, doughnut, globe, clock, earth, planet, ball.
1. *Similar-Sound Cues:* bun, fun, gun, none, won, one, pun, bunny, money, sunny.
   Symbol Cues: $1. dollar bill, route 1, 1 o'clock, 1 God, look-alike letter I.
2. *Similar-Sound Cues:* blew, blue, boo, two, too, to, chew, new, woo, drew.

Symbol Cues: 2 eyes, ears, hands, 2 anything; couple, twins.

3. *Similar-Sound Cues:* be, bee, fee, flea, three, see, she, tree, tea, plea, pea.

   Symbol Cues: 3M, triplets, trinity, triangle, triad, 3 of anything.

4. *Similar-Sound Cues:* for, door, nor, or, Thor, four, core, whore, more pour.

   Symbol Cues: "fore!" (golf), ford (4 wheels), quadruplets, 4 corners.

5. *Similar-Sound Cues:* Clive, I've, thrive, wives, dive, dives, cry, cries, five.

   Symbol Cues: a nickel, $5, 5 Great Lakes, hand (5 fingers), quintuplets.

6. *Similar-Sound Cues:* fix, mix, sticks, six, tricks, bricks, Styx, licks, ticks.

   Symbol Cues: 6 shooter, 6 pack, 6th floor, 6 cylinders, ½ dozen sticks.

7. *Similar-Sound Cues:* heaven, leaven, Kevin, Bevin, Previn, Stephan, Levin, seven.

   Symbol Cues: 7-up, a week (7 days), 7 o'clock, 7 wonders of the world.

8. *Similar-Sound Cues:* ate, hate, bait, eight, crate, fate, date, freight, gate.

   Symbol Cues: octagon, octopus, 8 cylinders, 8-ball.

9. *Similar-Sound Cues:* fine, Klein, line, mine, signs, nine, knife, Nile.

   Symbol Cues: baseball (9 on team), cat (9 lives), 9 lbs., age 9.

10. *Similar-Sound Cues:* Ben, ten, hen, Ken, men, pen, then, tent, went, yen, zen.

    Symbol Cues: a dime, a $10 bill, 10%, decade, tent, tennis, tentacle.

20. *Similar-Sound Cues:* plenty, Wendy, Benny, Jenny, Kenny, Lenny, many, penny, twenty.

    Symbol Cues: $20 bill, 20 lashes, 20/20 (glasses).

30. *Similar-Sound Cues:* dirty, Gertie, thirty, birdie, 3030 = dirty birdie or hurdy gurdy.

    Symbol Cues: a month, age 30, 30 degrees, 30 inches, 30 lbs.

40. *Similar-Sound Cues:* short, Morty, sortee, Fort E, forty, four
4   0
boats, more oats.
    Symbol Cues: 40 minutes, 40 years, 4 teas.

5   0

50. *Similar-Sound Cues:* nifty, shifty, fifty, thrifty, live oats, dive over.
    Symbol Cues: 50 states, 50¢, half-century, 50/50, 50%, 50 minutes.

60. *Similar-Sound Cues:* Trixie, sixty, Dixie, pixie, mix tea.
    Symbol Cues: 2 months (60 days), age 60, 60 miles per hour.

SAMPLE LISTING OF VARIOUS NUMBER SYMBOL CUES

007: James Bond.
107: 10 bottles of 7-up.
120: One dozen doughnuts (0 for doughnuts).
212: 212 degrees—boiling point of water.
98.6: a thermometer (normal body temperature in degrees).
180: 180 degrees in a straight line.
500: Fortune 500 companies, Indianapolis 500, $500.
710: Seven hens, seven dimes, 71 doughnuts.
747: Jetliner.
911: Police (emergency phone number).
1492: Columbus, 14 ninety-two-year-olds.
1600: White House (1600 Pennsylvania Ave., Washington, D.C.).
1776: a firecracker (Declaration of Independence—July 4).
1787: The Constitution (drafted in 1787).
1984: George Orwell's famous book title.
2001: The movie of that title.
5,280: A mile (5,280 feet).
20,000: book—"Twenty Thousand Leagues under the Sea."
25,000: Earth circumference.
186,000: an electric light bulb (the speed of light in miles per second).

Mathematics

The most sensible way to memorize or remember math

formulas, equations, and concepts is to understand them and apply them. The more you use them, the better you remember them. But if you decide that you need specific memory aids for extra assurance with these materials, the following ideas will help you.

Here are a few such examples, using cued sentences as always:

- *To Find the Area of a Square:*
  (b = length of side)
  (a = area)
  a = b²

Memory Cue: In this <u>area</u>, we'll all <u>be</u> <u>square</u>.
    (or)   <u>Bees</u> in this <u>area</u> are <u>square</u>.
    (or)   <u>Bears</u> are <u>squares</u> in this <u>area</u>.

- *To Find the Area of a Circle:*
  (r = radius)
  (pi is 3.1416)
  area = πr²

Memory Cue: In the <u>circled</u> <u>area</u>, <u>pies</u> <u>are</u> <u>square</u>.

- *To Find the Area of a Triangle:*
  (b = base)
  (h = vertical height)
  a = ½ bh

Memory Cue: The <u>triangular area</u> takes up <u>½</u> of <u>B</u>lue
                        <u>H</u>eaven.

- *To Find the Area of a Sphere:*
  (r = radius)
  area = 4πr²

                   area   sphere
Memory Cue: <u>Larry uh</u>, <u>fears</u> that <u>four pies are square</u>.

- *To Find the Volume of a Cube:*
(s = sides)
volume = s^3

$$\text{cube} \quad \text{volume} \qquad \text{s}$$

Memory Cue: <u>Cuba's volcano</u> lava <u>es</u>capes <u>three</u> times.

ALPHABETICAL LETTERS
USED IN FORMULAS AND EQUATIONS

Since alphabetical letters are used in formulas and equations, here is a table of Letter-Sound /Symbol Cues you can use for handy reference when you need them.

Letter	Cue
A	Ape
B	Bee
C	<u>Sea</u>
D	Deed
E	Eel
F	<u>Effort</u> (visualize a weightlifter expending <u>Effort</u> as he lifts.)
G	G—string, a <u>Gene</u>, or a <u>Jee</u>p
H	H—Bomb
I	Ice
J	Jay
K	Kay, Kate, or <u>Kite</u>
L	E<u>l</u>evator
M	E<u>m</u>peror
N	E<u>n</u>gine
O	Opal, Oboe
P	Pea
Q	Queue, or Cue
R	A<u>rm</u>y
S	E<u>s</u>kimo
T	Tea
U	Uke, U-boat

Letter	*Cue*
V	Venus
W	Double-hue (rainbow)
X	X-Ray, Eggs
Y	YMCA
Z	Zebra

This number memory system is covered in much greater detail in the author's previous book, *You Can Have a Near-Perfect Memory* (Chicago: Contemporary Books, Inc., 1982).

7

English Vocabulary

Looking up new words in the dictionary is no guarantee that you will remember the definitions. A dictionary is like school; it gives you the facts, but doesn't show you how to remember them. You can overcome this lack by immediate memory cueing of any new words that you wish to learn and remember.

Let's take an example—the word *perquisite*. As you may know, it means benefits or privileges over and above the usual. If the word perquisite was meaningless to you, it had the same effect on you as seeing or hearing a meaningless number for the first time. So the first thing to do, as always, is to cue that word with something that *sounds* and/or looks like it. Two such words that occur to me now are *perk* and *exquisite*. Now all we have to do is connect the original word with *perk* and *exquisite* into a cued sentence that includes the *meaning* of the new term. Here's the procedure, step by step:

Word to Learn	Similar Sound and/or Look-Alike Cue	Definition	Cued Sentence
perquisite	perk and exquisite.	privileges over and above the usual.	Perquisites perk me up for exquisite benefits and bonuses.

Now that we have cued it, it is reviewed a few times to let it sink in. After this, the best review for remembering new words is to use them as soon as you can in conversation. Use is the best stimulus for memory retention.

Let's take another word—pernicious. It means ruinous, hurtful, injurious, or wicked. Fern rhymes with the first syllable of the new word, and *vicious* rhymes with the last two syllables. With this in mind, you can come up with the sentence, "Fern is vicious and pernicious." Of course, not all words lend themselves to such perfect rhymes, but as you know by now, a perfect rhyme isn't at all necessary. Any similar-sound cue will do if it can remind you of the original word. For example, another perfectly serviceable sound cue for pernicious is *furnish us,* and your cued sentence this time might be:

"Things *pernicious furnish us* the *vicious,* and *dish us* hurt." The last four words are not really necessary, but they furnish an extra sound cue plus more meaning.

The vocabulary words on page 39 will illustrate further this simple, commonsense process. If you memorize each cue sentence by reciting and absorbing, you can test yourself at the end. You'll be delighted at the new words you have added to your present vocabulary. Also notice that it is not always necessary to include the original word as part of the cued sentence.

Word	Similar-Sound Cue	Definition	Cued Sentence
aberrant	Abner ran	deviation from what is considered normal or right.	Abner ran, showing strange behavior.
amicable	am I capable	exhibiting friendliness and good-will.	Am I capable of being friendly?
bel canto	Belle can totally	a smooth, sweet style of singing.	Belle can totally bewitch with her sweet singing.
maturation	mature nation or Matt, your nation	the process of becoming mature.	Matt, your nation is mature.
profligate	prof - gate	utterly and shamelessly reckless, immoral, or extravagant.	The prof got the gate because he was immoral.
stratagem	that's a gem	a ruse or trick to gain advantage.	That's a gem—a strategy for our advantage.
thesaurus	Tess or us	a specialized or comprehensive reference book.	Tess or us will read that Thesaurus.
travesty	Travis teed	a burlesque of serious work or subject.	Travis teed me off with his burlesque.
oxymoron	oxy moron	contradictory phrase such as "make haste slowly," or cruel kindness.	That oxy moron made haste slowly.
myopic	my optic	nearsighted.	My optic nerves are nearsighted.
convoluted	convoy looted	twisted, complicated, involved.	The convoy looted everything, twisting and turning everywhere.
deleterious	Della's serious	injurious to health; hurtful, harmful.	Della's serious; she'll hurt or harm anything.
calumny	call on me	false and malicious statement.	Don't call on me to make false statements.

THE METHOD IN A NUTSHELL

Cue It

1. To learn a new vocabulary word in English, think of another word or phrase that *sounds* like the new term, or that is similar to at least a main part of the new word.

2. Form a short phrase or sentence that includes the similar-sound cue with the meaning of the new word, and if possible, the new word itself. If you can mentally picture the interaction of the words in the sentence, so much the better as far as your memory is concerned.

Review It

Say the phrase or sentence a few times to commit it to memory. Then use every new word thus learned as early and as often as you can in your conversation and thinking. This will transfer it to your permanent vocabulary and keep it accessible to voluntary recall.

8

Foreign Language Vocabulary

Words in foreign languages are memorized in exactly the same way as are words in English. To your mind and memory, a strange foreign word is no different from a strange new word in English. Either one is a meaningless sequence of letters until *you* furnish the right cues and connections. Just be sure you first know the correct pronunciation and meaning; then you cue it and review it. The following examples will show you how to learn and memorize words in French, Spanish, Italian, and German.

FRENCH

Word	Similar-Sound Cue	Definition	Cued Sentence
eau (oh!)	Oh!	water	Oh! I want some water.
livre (leev-ra)	libra (sign of zodiac)	book	Libra is in the book.

Word	Similar-Sound Cue	Definition	Cued Sentence
usine (u-zeen)	using	factory	Using the factory is productive.
drapeau (drah-poe)	drop old	flag	Drop old flags.
stylo (stee-lo)	steal old	pen	Steal old pens.
dind (dand)	Dan (a first name)	turkey	Dan is a dandy turkey.
ecrire (ay-creer)	career	to write	A career in writing.
sur (soor)	sir	over	Sir, it's all over!
negliger (neg-lee-zhai)	negligee	overlook	The negligee was overlooked.

SPANISH

Word	Similar-Sound Cue	Definition	Cued Sentence
caro (cah-roe)	car, oh!	expensive	That car, oh, how expensive!
gripe (gree-pay)	agree to pay	flu	I agree to pay for a flu shot.
duro (doo-ro)	to row	hard	To row is hard.
campo (cahm-po)	calm pole	field	A calm Pole is in the field.
ojo (oh-ho)	Oh-ho!	eye	Oh-ho! You touched my eye.
hoy (oi)	toy	today	Buy a toy today.

Word	Similar-Sound Cue	Definition	Cued Sentence
comida (co-mee-da)	go meet her	dinner	Go meet her for dinner.
charco (char-co)	charcoal	puddle	The charcoal fell in the puddle.
tonto (ton-toe)	Tonto (Indian friend of Lone Ranger)	fool	Tonto was a fool.

ITALIAN

Word	Similar-Sound Cue	Definition	Cued Sentence
poco (po-co)	poke	little	Poke him a little.
forte (for-tay)	Fort "A"	loud	Fort "A" had a loud explosion.
giovane (joe-vahn)	Joe wants	young	Joe wants to be young.
apertura (ah-per-tiu-ra)	aperture	opening	The aperture is opening.
cappa (cah-pah)	copper	cloak	The copper wore a cloak.
mento (men-toe)	meant to	chin	I meant to chin myself.
sereno (seh-ren-o)	serene	cloudless	The sky was serene and cloudless.
freddo (fred-do)	Alfredo	cold	Alfredo is cold.
rapido (ra-pee-do)	repeat "Oh"	fast, quick	Repeat "Oh" quickly.

GERMAN

Word	Similar-Sound Cue	Definition	Cued Sentence
bitten (bit-ten)	bitten	request	He was bitten by request!
band (bond)	bond	ribbon	The bond was made by a ribbon.
befriedigen (be-freed-i-gen)	be freed again	satisfy	To be freed again is satisfying.
untertasse (oon-ter-ta-sai)	under Tessie	saucer	Under Tessie lies the saucer.
schere (sha-ra)	share the	scissors	Please share the scissors.
etwas (et-vas)	it was	something	It was really something!
fleck (flek)	flick	spot, stain	Flick the spot to remove the stain.
muster (moo-ster)	rooster	specimen	That rooster is a fine specimen.
essen (es-sen)	essence	to eat	The essence of life is to eat.

9
Literature

Names of books, authors, characters, quotes, and other types of literary information are not only good to know for their own sake, but this kind of material invariably shows up in exams. Naturally, you will remember a good many names, facts, plots, and other information you read—without the need for help in memorizing. But when you're under pressure with tons of books to read, deadlines to meet, and personal problems to boot, some good memory cueing can really help with special items you single out for this extra learning leverage.

As you read, mark the specific points or passages you feel will need cueing; either cue and recite it then and there, or come back later on, find your marks, and begin your cueing then. Some items will need very little repetition. Others may take a little more work until they sink in, ready for reproduction by heart. As we mentioned before, you will find that with a bit of practice, memory cueing is not only faster and far more reliable than the usual rote repetition method, but also it can be enjoyable and creative.

The following selections are taken from world literature. (Not the cues—the books.) Most of the memory cues themselves have been created during the writing of this book. Others are either well-known memory aids or cues given to me by students and teachers.

BOOKS AND AUTHORS

Book	Author	Memory Cues
Rosseau and Romanticism	Irving Babbit	Babbit was a romantic (Rousseau) rabbit—with a trousseau.
Huckleberry Finn	Mark Twain	Huck Finn rode on the Twain.
Gargantua and Pantagruel	Rabelais	Rabelais gargled and panted.
The Good Earth	Pearl Buck	The Good Earth was covered with Buckskin.
The Advancement of Learning	Sir Francis Bacon	Bacon was fakin' the advancement of learning.
Chéri	Colette	Cool it, Chéri!
Oliver Twist	Dickens	Who the Dickens wrote Oliver Twist?
Wuthering Heights	Emily Brontë	Would 'er thing hide in the brown hay?
A Fable for Critics	Lowell	There's a table for critics on the lower level.
Drum Taps	Walt Whitman	A dummy taps on the wall for a hit-man.
Barry Lyndon	Thackeray	Barry Lyndon thwacked away.
A Room of One's Own	Virginia Woolf	A Room of One's Own for the virgin wolf.

Book	Author	Memory Cues
Uncle Tom's Cabin	Harriet Beecher Stowe	Harriet beached the stowaway in Uncle Tom's Cabin.
Alexander's Feast	John Dryden	Alexander feasted while the john dried.
The Silent Woman	Ben Jonson	The silent woman has 'ben with John's son!
Barchester Towers	A. Trollope	Barchester Towers is haunted by a trollop.
Famous prose pamphlet *Areopagitica,* which resisted restriction of freedom of the press.	Milton	Milton pressed for freedom, sang an (Areo - pag - i - tica) aria, and patched his teacup.

AUTHORS AND THE CENTURIES IN WHICH THEY LIVED

Author	Century	Memory Cue
Charles Farrar Browne	19th	Charles, the far out brownie, had 19 cents. (nineteenth century)
Samuel Butler	19th	Samuel Butler had fine teeth sent. or Samuel Butler had a fine, keen scent.
Jeremy Taylor	17th	17 Jeremy's tailor had a heavenly sheen.
Edward Gibbon	18th	18 Edward ate tea with a Gibbon.

A LITTLE MORE PRACTICE
IN CUEING COMPLETE NAMES

Any name can be cued so that you can remember it. Some are easier than others, because they have better cueing potential, but the point is that if you really *observe* the name and take it syllable by syllable—and let your imagination run free —you can come up with workmanlike and reliable name cues when you need them. Similar-sound cues can be added *after* a name—or the *name itself* can become one.

Complete Name	*Full Name Cue*
Blaise Pascal	Blaze of pastel.
Thomas Robert Malthus	Thomas the robber had a malt on us.
Saul Bellow	Bald fellow.
John Bunyan	John Bunyan had a bunion.
Miguel de Cervantes	Make well the servants.
William Makepeace Thackeray	William made his peace, but thwacked Ray.

Some people have first and last names that are instantly meaningful and mentally picturable in themselves. For example, one of my recent memory seminar students was Warren Peese, an architect. As soon as I heard his name, I thought of Tolstoy's book, *War and Peace,* and I pictured the book on top of a *skyscraper* as a symbol cue for architect. In this way, *War and Peace* on a *skyscraper* became a full name cue and occupation cue, and I can still remember that gentleman.

Three other such names I can recall from my classes were Otto Horne, Lauren Mauer, and Violet Organ. I cued Otto Horne as *auto horn,* Lauren Mauer as *lawn mower,* and Violet Organ as a *violet organ.*

Whenever you wish to cue complete names, the first step is to try to recognize the possibilities in the names themselves. It's not enough just to read them or hear them; you must *observe* them.

> You see and hear
> With your eye and ear
> But you only observe with the mind.

By observing names, you can discover various possibilities that might otherwise remain hidden. As an example, here are some currently notable names from the theater, cinema, literature, and sports. The following full name cues were created by some of my students when they were asked to observe these names.

Name	Full Name Cue
Jack Lemmon	Cash for lemons
Marlon Brando	A marlin drinking brandy
Gore Vidal	A bore withal
Luciano Pavarotti	Lucy on a paved potty
Cloris Leachman	Clorox bleach
John Voight	Toilet empty
Robert Redford	Robber in a red Ford
George Burns	George burns
Muhammad Ali	More ham in the alley

CHARACTERS IN BOOKS

Character	Book	Cue
Malambruno	*Don Quixote* (Kee-ho-tay)	Madam Bruno is down in the keyhole. (It goes without saying that whenever you cue a full name, you must remember that the cue is not the name, but a *reminder* of that name.)

Character	Book	Cue
Long John Silver	*Treasure Island*	Long John found Silver on Treasure Island.
Lotus-eaters	*The Odyssey*	Lotus-eaters are odd, see?
John Ridd	*Lorna Doone*	John got rid of Lorna Doone.
Charles Honeyman	*The Newcomes*	Charlie's a honeyman with a new comb.
Miss Flite	*Bleak House*	Miss Flite was a sight in her bleak house.
Kenyon	*Marble Faun*	In the canyon was a marble faun.
Mahbub Ali	*Kim*	Mah buddy, Ali, in a kimono.
Aunt Polly	*Tom Sawyer*	Aunt Polly said Tom saw her.

Cues are reminders, and this is our cue to remind you that the purpose of all the examples is to show you some of the many ways that memory cueing can be done. No one way is necessarily "correct." What *you* think up, and what *you* feel would work best for you, is always the best one to use.

Character	Book	Cue
Mark Rampion	*Point Counter Point*	Mark, the champion, countered a point.
Kate Croy	*Wings of a Dove*	Kate and Croy flew on the wings of a dove.
Private Carr	*Ulysses*	A private car—you'll see!
Bigger Thomas	*Native Son*	The bigger Thomas, the bigger his native son.
John Thornton	*The Call of the Wild*	Thorny John called wildly.

POEMS AND POETS

Poem	Author	Cue
"Columbus"	Joaquin Miller	Columbus had a cup of joe at the tiller.
"Merchants from Cathay"	W. R. Benet	Merchants from Cathay (W. R. Benet) doubled our benefits.
"Brotherhood"	Edwin Markham	Brother Edwin marked a ham.
"I Have a Rendezvous with Death"	Allan Seeger	"I have a rendezvous with death," said Al, the seeker.

CHARACTERS IN SHAKESPEARE'S PLAYS

Character	Play	Cue
Bottom	Midsummer Night's Dream	Bottom reached bottom on a summer night.
Cordelia	King Lear	"Cordelia, I want to steal 'ya," said the king, with a leer.
Wolsey	Henry the Eighth	Wolsey said, "See what Henry ate?"
Belmont	Merchant of Venice	Belmont rang the bell for the merchant of Venice.
Sardis	Julius Caesar	"Sorry, 'dis Caesar cat must go!"
Angelo	Othello	The Angel of Jello.
Falstaff	Merry Wives of Windsor	Falstaff falls on the Merry Wives.

WHICH PLAYS PRODUCED
SHAKESPEARE'S FAMOUS QUOTES

Quote	Play	Cue
"To thine own self be true."	Hamlet	To thine own self be true, and thee won't be a <u>ham</u>.
"The course of true love never did run smooth."	Midsummer Night's Dream	The course of <u>true love</u> <u>never did run smooth</u> on a <u>midsummer night</u>.
"Cowards die many times before their death."	Julius Caesar	<u>Cowards die many times</u> <u>before their death</u>—in <u>Caesar's</u> freezer.
"We are such stuff as dreams are made."	The Tempest	<u>We are such stuff as dreams</u> <u>are made</u>, especially when they are<u> tempting</u>.
"All the world's a stage."	As You Like It	<u>All the world's a stage</u>—if <u>you like it</u>.

Although you should not spend an excessive amount of time in creating your cues, remember that the more memorable the cue is itself, the better and longer it will be able to remind you of the information it holds. That's why a little humor, coincidence, or even the ridiculous can be powerful cueing ingredients—to trigger and revive the original memory impression.

10

Music

Memory cueing has been used to teach the elements of music by almost every music teacher at one time or another. Music is one of the few subjects in which we were taught not only what to know, but also *how to remember it.*

As mentioned in a previous chapter, a good example of this is the way the lines and spaces of the music staff have been taught to us. The treble staff lines, E,G,B,D,F, were meaningless until they were cued into a meaningful sentence as *E*very *G*ood *B*oy *D*oes *F*ine. Do you still remember this? You probably also remember the four spaces of the staff, F, A, C, and E, as the one word cue, FACE. Even people who are not musicians, who learned these things as children, still remember them today. This was good memory cueing indeed.

Other cues for the ledger lines above and below the treble and bass are also used. Some of them are as follows:

- The 3 ledger lines above the treble staff—A, C, and E— become ACE.
- The 3 spaces above the treble staff—G, B, and D—become *G*reat *B*ull *D*og, *G*reat *B*ig *D*ippers, or whatever other cues are created.
- The 5 lines of the bass staff—G,B,D,F, and A—are usually cued as *G*ood *B*oys *D*o *F*ine *A*lways.
- The 4 spaces of the bass staff—A,C,E,G—are usually remembered as *A*ll *C*ows *E*at *G*rass.

If you sing in a choir, you can quickly recall the four sections or voice ranges as STAB (*S*oprano, *T*enor, *A*lto, *B*ass). I was a music major in college, and I still remember the main periods in music history because of a letter-cue sentence I made up at that time. The periods in sequence are:

Antiquity, Polyphonic, Baroque, Classical, Romantic, Modern, and Contemporary. I cued these into a sentence as *A*ll *P*eriods *B*ecome *C*lassified *R*egarding *M*ost *C*omposers, and I still remember my music history. Without these cues, I could probably mentally reconstruct this sequence of periods by reasoning alone. But it's so much easier and *faster* with the aid of that simple sentence cue—even today, after all these years.

If I knew then what I know now, I think I would have cued the music history periods with similar-sound cues instead of letter cues. It might have been something like:

Aunt Polly's *Bar* was *Classy*
with *Romantic Mod*els—*Con*stipated.

But I certainly can't complain, because the letter cues still do their duty.

If you are a music student, you may want to remember the six ancient modes in music: Ionian, Dorian, Phrygian, Lydian, Mixo-lydian, and Aolian. If so, here are two types of cues, either of which will do the job. Learn it, review it, and you'll keep it.

• *I own Dor*a's *Fridge*, but *Lydia Mix*es *Oleo*. (Oleo will remind you of Aolian if you originally connect it this way.)

• IDPLMA! This is such a ridiculous word, that you'll remember it. Each letter, of course, stands for a separate ancient mode.

Music lovers who can't remember the four sections of the symphony orchestra (strings, woodwinds, brass, percussion) can easily recall this sequence with *String* up the *Woodwinds* in a *Brass Perc*olator!

MUSIC TERMINOLOGY

The universal language in music is Italian. For quick memorization of many music terms, you can cue them with similar sounds as follows:

Term	English Similar Sound	English Translation	Memory Cue
poco a poco	poke	little by little	Poke him, little by little.
forte (for-tay)	fort A	loud	Fort A had a loud explosion.
rapido (ra-pee-do)	rapid	fast, quick	Rapid.
largo	Margo	slowly and stately	Margo is slow, but stately.
piano	piano	soft	The piano plays softly.
agitato (aj-i-tah-to)	agitated	agitated	Aggie is agitated.
dolce (dol-chay)	dole	sweetly	Dole pineapple juice is sweet.

Term	English Similar Sound	English Translation	Memory Cue
vivace (viv-ah-chay)	vivacious	vivacious	Vivacious.
molto	mold	much	The mold is too much.
maestoso (mice-toso)	mice toes	majestically	Mice on my toes are majestic.

Reminder: So many terms, facts, and other types of information can be learned and remembered by themselves, with no memory aids whatsoever. Common sense dictates that memory cues are to be used only when needed.

OPERAS AND COMPOSERS

Opera	Composer	Memory Cue
Vanessa	Samuel Barber	In the Van is Sam, the Barber
Lulu	Alban Berg	Lulu had an all-bran burger.
Prince Igor	Borodin	Prince Igor burrowed in.
Martha	von Flotow	Martha is von good floater!
Porgy and Bess	Gershwin	Porgy said, "Gosh, I win!"
Les Huguenots	Meyerbeer	The Huguenots and Meyer had beer.
The Impressario	Mozart	The Impressario likes Moe's art.
The Magic Flute	Mozart	The Magic Flute played Mozart.

Opera	*Composer*	*Memory Cue*
Madama Butterfly	Puccini	<u>Madame Butterfly</u> had a <u>pooch</u>.
The Bartered Bride	Smetana	<u>The Bartered Bride</u> was <u>smitten</u>.
Elektra	Richard Strauss	The <u>electric</u> mouse Of <u>Richard Strauss</u>.
The Rake's Progress	Stravinsky	<u>The Rake Progressed</u>, strapped in a <u>ski</u>.
Falstaff	Verdi	<u>Falstaff</u> sings like a <u>birdie</u>.
Tristan und Isolde	Wagner	<u>Tristan und Isolde</u> went on the <u>wagon</u>.

11
Basic Psychology

All learning is based on memory, and the things that current research stresses for efficient learning—attentiveness, imagery, organization of material, association, and meaning —are the elements you are deliberately using for the creation and use of memory cues. The study of psychology encompasses all activities and processes of the brain, so it is entirely appropriate that we now apply the ideas and techniques of memory and cueing to psychology itself.

We will start with some items of terminology and progress to a few general facts and concepts, each of which will be cued for easier memorization.

REMEMBERING TERMINOLOGY

Term to Memorize	Definition	Memory Cue
		(En - ur - resis)
Enuresis	Bed wetting	End your resistance, and stop wetting the bed.

Term to Memorize	*Definition*	*Memory Cue*
Fetish	Preference for an object rather than a person for sexual gratification.	<u>Fay's dish</u> is not men, but dishes.
Aphasia	Impairment or loss of ability to speak or write.	<u>Half of Asia</u> can't speak or write.
Autonomy	A sense of independence, of being an individual separate from other people.	(au - to - no - my) I <u>aught to know myself</u> as an <u>independent individual</u>.
Diathesis	A genetic predisposition to a particular psychotic disorder.	<u>Diane's thesis</u> is on <u>genetically inclined psychosis</u>.

REMEMBERING FACTS

Fact to Memorize	*Memory Cue*
The Seashore battery of tests measures musical talent.	<u>Seashore</u> displays <u>musical talent</u> on the seashore.
Tolman's experiment in purposive behavior was of maze-learning by rats.	<u>Tolman's</u> <u>purposive behavior</u> amazed rats.
"The Psychology Of Adjustment" was written by Shaffer.	"<u>The Psychology Of Adjustment</u>" was written with a <u>Sheaffer</u> pen.
William Wundt, founder of Structuralism, concluded that the three elements of mind are sensations, images, and feelings.	<u>Wundt's</u> structured conclusion was to "<u>S</u>end 'im a fee." (<u>S</u>ensations, <u>I</u>mages, <u>F</u>eelings)
Freud's psychoanalytic theory involved three personality structures: Id, Ego, Superego.	<u>Freud's id</u>—'<u>e go</u> on a <u>superego</u> trip. (or)

Fact to Memorize	*Memory Cue**
	IES (I's) a monster! (Id, Ego, Superego)
Four varieties of schizophrenia are: Simple, Paranoid, Hebephrenic, and Catatonic.	Simple paranoids have Hebrew cats. (or) Si, Pa! He got that cat a tonic. (or) See Pa—he cat! (or) SIPA-HECAT ("Word" letter cue) As you can see, sometimes cue possibilities are so varied that your creative powers can go on a binge, as in the last example. When this happens, write them all down and select the best one.
Three measures of central tendency in elementary statistics are Mean, Median, and Mode.	I measured your central tendencies and you are mean mediocre, and outmoded. (or) Statistically, mean mediums have pie a la mode. (or) You're mean, but I'd mediate if you mowed. (or) The mean median was mowed.
Three primary defense mechanisms are denial, repression, and isolation.	The defense was DRI. (Denial, Repression, Isolation) (or) In defense, I deny and repress my isolation.

Fact to Memorize	*Memory Cue*
Eight secondary defense mechanisms are: <u>dis</u>placement, <u>pro</u>jection, <u>id</u>entification, <u>ra</u>tionalization, <u>intel</u>lectualization, <u>subs</u>titution, <u>fan</u>tasy, and re<u>gre</u>ssion.	'Dis <u>pro</u> identifies <u>ra</u>tional <u>intel</u>ligence and <u>subs</u>titutes <u>fan</u>cy re<u>gre</u>ts. (If you prefer the brevity of letter cues, any of the following may suffice: DRIP SIRF / FIR DRIPS / DR. FRISIP / DR. F. PISIR / IF DR. RIPS / I.R. DR. SIP / DR. SIP FRI

THE SCIENTIFIC METHOD

General procedures involved in scientific observation are:

1. Collect and record facts accurately and systematically.
2. Analyze and evaluate them.
3. Share the final data and conclusions with others in the field.
4. Add and relate the new findings to previous knowledge.
5. Provide subsequent researchers with a better start.

After careful reading and understanding of this kind of information, you may still want to memorize it for systematic recall. With the above, you can do this quite efficiently in three ways:

1. The similar-sound cued sentence: *Scientific, Cold Anna Shares* and *Adds Prov*isions.
2. The letter cue C A S A P.
3. An advanced memory cue method you will learn in Chapter 16.

12

Biology, Genetics, and Anthropology

As always, learning the terminology of any subject is the first key to its mastery. Understanding the terms enables you to follow your instructor and to grasp what you are reading or studying. In previous pages you learned how to simplify learning and remembering new words by cueing them. Although there still is no substitute for good concentrated study, the intelligent use of good memory cues will not only speed up your learning time, but can give you the confidence of control—especially at exam time—which you may not have experienced before. First choose the specific information you want to memorize; next take the small amount of time necessary to create your cues. Then review and recite to memorize the cues. After this, merely go over your cues once in a while. You can literally *file them* for mental reviews with the mental filing system taught in Chapter 16.

REMEMBERING TERMINOLOGY

Term	Definition	Cue
nomenclature (no-men-klay-cher)	The inclusion of both terms and names in a particular subject.	No men claim stature without a name.
Afferent neurons and Efferent neurons	Afferent are incoming signals to the brain. Efferent are outgoing signals from the brain.	After coming in, it's an Effort to go out. (or) After in—Effort out.
Paleontology	The study of fossils.	Pale Leon, tall and logy, is a fossil.
Morphology	The study of structure of organisms.	More follow Jean—to study her structure.

REMEMBERING CLASSIFICATIONS, FACTS, AND PROCESSES

In biology, one of the basic things you must know is the hierarchical organization of animal classification. First you should know the meaning of each category term, and then the established hierarchical sequence.

Term and Meaning	Memory Cues
Kingdom of Animals and Plants	K A P
Phylum: Chordata	File 'em according to data.
Class: (Mammalia)	Momma Lea has class!
Order: (Carnivora)	Order at the carnival.
Family: (Canidae)	The family went to Canida.
Genus: (*Canis*)	Genius can itch!
Species: (*Familiars*)	Specify the familiar.

It is always interesting (and important) to note how quickly such memory cues can be memorized, and how easily you

can recall the coded information. One of the best character-
istics of this memory method is that when you review and
decode your cues once in a while, you will hardly need the
original cues anymore. You will just *know* the information.

Now let's take all seven hierarchical animal classifications
and quickly commit them to memory.

Terms: Kingdom, Phylum, Class, Order, Family, Genus, and
    Species.
Similar-Sound Cue: King Phylo's Class Orders the Family Genius
        to Speak.
Letter Cue: King Phillip Came Over From Germany Stoned.

In general, I recommend the similar-sound cue over the
letter cue. But they both work. It's up to you to choose, learn
them, and use them.

FACTS ABOUT BLOOD CHEMISTRY

Fact to Memorize	*Memory Cue*
Three basic blood cell types— erythrocytes, leukocytes, and thrombocytes.	Eric rows and sights Luke, who sights a trombone.
Antigen: a substance that stimu- lates formation of antibodies.	Auntie Gen stimulates Auntie's body.
Antibodies are found in plasma.	Auntie's body is in the plaza.
Plasma is serum with fibrinogen, a clotting mechanism.	In the plaza, I told a serious fib to Gen, about my clotting mechanism.

SEQUENCE OF NINE MENDELIAN TERMS IN GENETICS

Terms: genes, allele, locus, genotype, heterozygous, recessive,
    genetic dominance, phenotype, and segregation.
Similar-Sound Cues: Gene and Al were loco. But Geno's typists,
        Heather and Gus, recessed a genetic
        phenomenon, and then went to see Greg.

Once you know these two cued sentences, all you have to do is decode the key words during review. The sentences keep the information—in formation.

Fact to Memorize	*Memory Cues*
Three main areas of Genetics are Biochemical (molecular), Mendelian, and Population Genetics.	Biochemical moles mend their population.

The above three categories also serve to classify three aspects of the behavior of genes. Individually cued, they could be as follows:

Facts to Memorize	*Memory Cues*
A. *Biochemical:* What genes are and what they do.	Buy chemical jeans? What are they, and what do they do?
B. *Mendelian:* how genes are passed from one generation to the next.	Mendel and Gene created succeeding generations.
C. *Population Genetics:* how evolutionary forces change frequency of genes.	The population evolves and forces genies to change frequency.

Four basic kinds of change in organisms:
1. Reversible changes in individuals.
2. Developmental " " "
3. Cyclic " " "
4. Evolutionary changes in populations.

REV-DEV CYC-EVO
(or)
For a change, Reverse and Develop Evolving Cycles.

You could easily include the word *organisms* in the cues if you feel you need a more complete reminder. But remember that the better you understand the information itself, the shorter and simpler your cues can be.

Facts to Memorize	*Memory Cues*
Zygote: the product of fusion of sperm and ova.	Si got produced when sperm move ova.

Facts to Memorize	Memory Cue
Prezygote mechanisms prevent reproduction between species.	Prezygotes prevent "special" species.

In the study of cells, the four stages of Mitosis (division of cell nucleus) is of basic importance.

The four phases of Mitosis are: prophase, metaphase, anaphase, and telophase.	Mighty sis, a pro, met Ana on television.
Three flower reproductive structures: the stamen, anther, and pistil.	The stamen is the anther to the pistil's dreams.
Milk is exposed to ultraviolet light to increase the quantity of vitamin D.	When milk is exposed to Violet, it gets V.D.
Mammals include the vertebrate group to which whales belong.	Mamma-whale.
Pfaffman worked on the gustatory nerves in animals	Pfaffman liked gusto and nerve in animals.

ANTHROPOLOGY

Facts to Memorize	Memory Cue
Important scientists in Anthropology are Cuvier, Buffon, Lamarck, Lyell, Malthus, and Darwin.	Cover and Buff the Lamb with Lye and Malt for Darwin.
The five fossil races of man: Java Ape Man, Peking, Heidelberg, Neanderthal, and Cro-Magnon.	Flossy raced from Java to Peking, hiding Nina from the crows.

ERAS, PERIODS, AND EPOCHS
IN THE HISTORY OF THE EARTH

Eras: Archeozoic, Proterozoic, Paleozoic, Mesozoic, Cenozoic

Cues: Archie's stoic prototype pales, but it mesmerized the century.

Periods: Cambrian, Ordovician, Silurian, Devonian, Carboniferous, Permian, Triassic, Jurassic, Cretaceous, Tertiary, and Quarternary.

Cues: Camp Ordo's Silver Developed Carbon Perks when a Trial Jury of Cretins Turned Quarrelsome.

Epochs: Paleocene, Eocene, Oligocene, Miocene, Pliocene, Pleistocene, Recent.

Cues: The Pail seen by Eon, Ollie, and Mike was Plied with Plaster Recently.

As you can see, even seemingly difficult material lends itself to imaginative cueing. With a bit of review, such items are no more difficult to commit to memory than any other subject matter.

13

Physics

Remembering facts and figures is an important element in the field of physics. As you read through the following examples, keep in mind that the purpose of cueing is only to make needed and specific information easier to remember. We will cue various items of knowledge in astronomy, engineering, electricity, chemistry, and energy.

Fact to Memorize	*Cue*
Agassiz made his major contribution in the field of chemistry.	A gas is contributed in chemistry.
The forms of energy are: Mechanical, Chemical, Solar, Heat, Atomic, Light, and Electrical.	Energy from Mechanical Chemicals Sold, Heats up Atomic Electric Lights.
	(or)

Fact to Memorize	*Cue*

Letter Cues:

a. Must Chemical Smog Heat Adam's Live Electric Energy?

b. CLASH 'EM! (An "energetic" memory cue)

You can always change the sequence of items to fit your memory cue ideas—unless strict order is required. Remember that it is best if you can include the *subject* of the cue (in this case, Energy) in your cued sentence so there will be no mistake as to what the cue explains.

The Earth's diameter is 7,927 miles.

"Calling Earth 7, at 9:27. Do you read, Diane?" (diameter)

The Earth's circumference is 25,000 miles.

Circle the globe for only 25¢ per thousand miles.

The speed of light is 186,282 miles per second.

          1 8 6
With lightning speed I ate 6
      2/   82
bulbs in February of '82.

The distance of the moon from the Earth is 238,866 miles.

  2 38
Two 38s shot a bullet to the
     8   66
moon in August of '66.

The distance of the sun from the Earth is 93,000,000 miles.

Son, if you live to be 93, you'll be one in a million!

Formula for sulphuric acid: H_2SO_4

"Poor little Willie
He's not here no more
'Cause what he thought was H_2O
Was H_2SO_4"
        (An old mnemonic cue)

Fact to Memorize	*Cue*
It takes approximately 8 minutes for light from the sun to reach the Earth.	Change the L in Sun <u>L</u>ight to E, and you have Sun-<u>Eight.</u> (8 minutes). Also, there are <u>8 letters in Sunlight</u>. (8 letters = 8 minutes)
The four types of clouds are Cumulus, Stratus, Nimbus, and Cirrus.	<u>Cum</u>ulative <u>Stra</u>tas are <u>Nim</u>ble, <u>Sir</u> <u>Cloud</u>!
The cloud type that occurs at the greatest height is the Cirrus.	The <u>Cirrus</u> <u>high</u> wire act in the <u>clouds</u>.
One planet that can never be observed from Earth at night is Mercury.	At <u>night</u>, it's too murky to see <u>Mercury</u>.
The Earth revolves around the sun at about 66,000 miles per hour.	Q: Did you know the Earth circles the sun at 66,000 mph? A: Sure—it uses Phillips 66! (Sometimes a wisecrack can be so outlandish or corny that it can become an unforgettable memory cue. Use this idea for your cueing when appropriate.)
The maximum possible duration in minutes of a total solar eclipse at any one spot on Earth is about 7½ minutes.	In <u>minutes</u> we are <u>totally eclipsed</u> 7 ½ when <u>heaven hath</u> spoken.
The number of stars visible to the naked eye in both the north and south hemispheres is about 5,000.	<u>5</u> point stars, visible in the heavens. (or) (The words <u>north</u> and <u>south</u> each have 5 letters. 5 = 5,000)
The Earth's orbital velocity is 18½ miles per second.	You can <u>orbit</u> the <u>earth</u> for just <u>$18.50</u>.

Fact to Memorize	*Cue*
A cubic foot of water weighs 95 lbs.	From 9 to 5, I drank a cubic foot of water.

A mile equals 5,280 feet.

          5/2   80
I walked a mile on May 2, of '80.

1 nautical mile = 6076.1 feet.

         (sixty
Naughty Milo gave Trixie
  seventy-six   .1)
heavenly kicks-once.

The Aswan High Dam was built across the Nile River.

A swan flew across the damn Nile.

The formula for horsepower is Pressure × Length × Area × Number of Revolutions.

Letter Cue: PLAN for Horsepower.
        (or)
The Horse Presses Len into the Arena for a Number of Revolutions.

Mount Fujiama is 12,365 feet high.

It takes a year to climb Mount Fujiama!
(year = 12 months, or 365 days)

The planets in their order from the sun: Mercury, Venus, Earth, Mars, Jupiter, Saturn, Uranus, Neptune, and Pluto.

My Very Elegant Mother Just Served Us Nine Pizzas.
        (or)
Murky and Venal Eartha said that Marcy and June Sat on Ursula's Nephew, Pluto!

The International Electrical Color Code numbers resistors and capacitors worldwide. The colors in correct order are: Black-Brown-Red-Orange-Yellow-Green-Blue-Violet-Gray-White.

Bad Boys Ruin Our Young Girls, But Violet Gives Willingly.
        (or)
Blackie, a Brown & Red Orangutan, Yelled at Green while Violet turned Gray-White.

14

Law

STATUTES, DOCTRINES, TERMINOLOGY

The facts, concepts, and numbers involved in legal language and terminology can be considerably simplified for memorization through cueing and review. A few examples will show this.

Internal Revenue Statute number 368 has to do with definitions regarding corporate mergers, acquisitions, reorganizations, and consolidations.

Assuming that the legal student knows these statute examples are from the IRS code, we will cue the statute number and the five underlined concepts above, without reference to the IRS.

The first thing to do is to notice the built-in letter cues as follows: *M*ergers, *A*cquisitions, *R*eorganization, and *C*onsolidation = *MARC,* a short and serviceable letter-cue reminder. The similar-sound cue method, on the other hand,

72

would produce something like the following, with *sound cues* for recall:

Mergers Acquire Reorganized Consolidations.

Next, we take a look at the statute number 368, and it could be cued, say, as:

3   6   8
The fee fix is great (or 3/68—March of '68)

With such ideas we could then cue all of the material into any of these sentences:

- The *fee fix* is *great* for the *corporate MARC.*
- *In 3/68* the *mergers acquired reorganized consolidations.*
- For *$368* the *corporation merged* its *acquisitions* by *reorganizing* and *consolidating.*
- *Three sixty-eight*-year-old *corporate* executives made their *MARC.*
- *Three 6* foot *8 corporate MARCs.*

Another statute, number 213, refers to medical and dental deductions. Here are some examples for cueing this statute:

- 2   13
  Two flirting doctors and dentists are deductible.
- 2   1   3
  To one like me, medical and dental deductions are important.
- 213 pounds of receipts for medical and dental deductions!
- $2.13 is for medical and dental deductions.

The shorter the cues the better, as long as the power to remind you is there.

DOCTRINES OF LAW

The following are six important doctrines of law:

1. Assumption of Risk
2. Judicial Review
3. Consideration
4. Exclusionary Rule
5. Unconscionability
6. Clean Hands Doctrine

To remember them in order may not be necessary, but for now, we'll take them the way they come. Here's a simple memory cue that will bring this information back to you any time, any place:

I *assume, judge,* you will *consider excluding* me because I'm *unconscious* and I have *clean hands.*

It seems hard to imagine anything easier that would still work. Of course, if you know your doctrines, all you need is a letter cue in the form of the name, *A.J.CEUC.* Each letter, of course, cues its doctrine. But for *longer term* remembering, it's usually wiser to let the *similar-sound cue* practically tell you each item of information so cued, especially for lengthy material.

LEGAL TERMINOLOGY

Cueing in law works the same as with any other subject. The chart on page 75 illustrates a few legal terms and examples for good measure.

Term	Similar Sound	Definition	Memory Cue
abrogate	Ambrose's gate	To repeal or annul a law.	The <u>Ambrose gate</u> was painted, but it re-peeled.
caveat emptor	caviar empty	Let the buyer beware.	<u>Caviar is empty—beware, buyer!</u>
eleemosynary	Eli-mercenary	charitable	<u>Eli's not mercenary; he's chairing the table.</u>
lessee	let's see	He to whom a lease is made.	<u>Let's see</u> who gets the <u>lease.</u>
suit	suit	Any proceeding in court to recover a right or claim.	It <u>suits</u> me to claim my rights in <u>court.</u>
vendee	'Ven de . . . (When the . . .)	Person to whom a thing is sold. A buyer.	<u>'Ven de customer buys, it's sold.</u>

PART III:

REMEMBERING CONTINUITY, SEQUENCE, AND DETAIL

15

An Advanced Memory Cue System

Up to this point we have worked mainly with cueing and recalling specific facts in various fields of study. Now that you know the basics, you can organize this knowledge into a system that can handle the retention and recall of virtually any information.

You have learned to create and use Similar-Sound Cues, Letter Cues, and Multiple-Sentence Cues (Story Cues)—all in the form of the cued sentence.

Now you are going to use these techniques to construct an actual *mental filing system* which will retain and deliver back to you the continuity, sequence, and details of any material you file away for future retrieval. The basic idea is still the power of the versatile memory cue—which, once thought of, quickly triggers its related information back to mind.

The first ten amendments to the constitution—the Bill of Rights—contain information everyone should know. The first amendment reads as follows:

Congress shall make no law respecting an establishment of religion, or prohibiting the free exercise thereof; or abridging the freedom of speech, or of the press; or the right of the people peaceably to assemble, and to petition the Government for a redress of grievances.

Please notice that only the most important key points will be extracted for cueing. These key points are *freedom of religion, speech, the press,* and the right to *assemble* and *petition.*

Cueing this material into a sentence could easily result in the following:

Free religious speeches are *pressed* and *assembled* into *petitions.*

As always, you don't need the exact wording or even spelling of these key points as they appear in the original form. You can change the tense, the appearance, the sequence, the spelling, or whatever—*as long as the final result has the power to remind you of the original word and meaning.* Throughout this book you have been working basically with *reminders.* Remember the law of contiguity? It stated that any two things *experienced together* will become associated with each other in the mind so that one thing will remind you of the other. Your sentence cues provide you with all the associated reminders that you need to bring back the material memorized with those sentence reminder cues.

Now in the Bill of Rights, there are ten amendments, each of which may require one or more cued sentences. A few such sentences are not too difficult to remember; even a half-dozen or more of them, when strung into a story cue, can be committed to memory if you are able to spend the extra time. But organizing sentences into a story and then memorizing the sequence of those sentences can take too much time when you don't have it, and that's where advanced cueing with a mental file enters the picture.

The system you are about to learn bypasses the need for this kind of sequential "story form" sentence memorization, and accomplishes the same purpose more easily and quickly. With story-cue sentences, it is possible to forget a sentence, in which case the succeeding sentences may be lost. But this is highly unlikely with advanced cueing, as you will see. Although careful initial cueing is required, as always, you will then have *direct* mental access to each and every cued sentence mentally filed.

16

A New Mental Filing System

THE WORD OR PHRASE FILE

You will now learn to use your brain in much the same way that you would use a file cabinet. In an office, if you want to retain a letter from a Mr. Thomas for future retrieval, you go to the file drawer and file the letter (the information) under letter T. Later, when the need arises for that *T*homas information, the alphabet cue, T, tells you exactly where to find the information in the file, and you have no difficulty in retrieving it. During this complete process, you have *read* the letter, *filed it,* and successfully *retrieved* it. Similarly in mental filing, you *study and cue* the information you wish to memorize, *file it* in your mind in such a way that you know exactly how to get it back out again, and then—by thinking of the correct mental file cue—you *locate and retrieve* the information.

All you need to build a mental file is any word or phrase

with the same number of letters as the number of information units you wish to memorize. For example, the Bill of
Rights has ten amendments, so there would be ten information units to memorize. So to start a mental file, you need a
word or a phrase with exactly ten letters in all. The only other
requirement is that this mental file word or phrase should not
have any repeating letters in it. For example, the word *advance* cannot be used because the letter *a* appears more than
once in that word. Similarly, the words *condominium,
bazooka,* or the phrases *Hotel Elliot,* or *correct time* cannot
be used because of the repeated letters in those words or
phrases.

On the other hand, the words *plenty, picture, education,*
or *English* may each be used as a mental file because each
contains no repeated letters. Similarly, the phrases *four days,
in the dark, one track,* or *top drawer* can each be used as an
individual mental file—again because each phrase has no
repeated letters. So, to recap, the two requirements for a
word or phrase to become a mental file are:

1. It must have exactly the same number of letters as there
   are information units to memorize.
2. It should not have repeated letters.

With these simple requirements, we can now begin to
create a complete mental file for the Bill of Rights. Actually,
the phrase *Bill of Rights* itself would make an ideal mental
file if it didn't have the repeated letters, i and l. We need
something else with ten different letters. If you can come up
with a mental file word or phrase that is obviously related to
the type of information involved, so much the better—even
though this is not a requirement.

As for the Bill of Rights, if someone were to ask you to
"Name your Rights!"—you could take that phrase, drop the
word *your,* and just use NAME RIGHTS as the basis for the
mental file. NAME RIGHTS has ten letters, and they're all

different. Therefore we will use it to memorize the Bill of Rights.

Remember that:

- NAME RIGHTS is the *mental file phrase.*
- Each letter in NAME RIGHTS is a *mental file cue.*

17

Memorizing the Bill of Rights

In Chapter 15 we cued the key points from the first amendment—freedom of religion, speech, the press, and the right to assemble and petition—into the sentence:

Free religious speeches are *pressed* and *assembled* into *petitions.*

Now we're going to *mentally file* this cued sentence with *N*—the first file cue in the file *NAME RIGHTS.* When you pronounce the letter N, it sounds like *en,* so we will simply use the sound "en" to connect the file cue N to the cued sentence. You do this by simply thinking of any word you like that *starts* with the sound *en.* It's easy—*en*d, *en*gineer, *en*dear, *en*tire, *en*tertain, *en*tire, *en*sign, *en*trance, *en*ergy, *en*chant—any one you like. The word *en*gineer is concrete and pictureable, so we will use it.

$$N = engineer.$$

Make that simple connection, and remember it now.

Now, with a slight change in wording the former cued sentence can become:

*En*gineers make *free religious speeches* and *assemble pressed partitions.*

Get the idea? Since we now began the sentence with *Engineer,* such minor changes make for a better and more memorable cue sentence.

Now repeat this sentence a few times until you know it cold—without having to look at it:

*En*gineers make *free religious speeches* and *assemble pressed partitions.*

As things stand now, all you have to do in order to recall the entire first amendment is to merely think of the first letter of your mental file, *N*AME RIGHTS. Then the sound cue *En* will trigger *Engineers,* and the complete cued sentence will flash to mind, with all the freedoms and rights in the same package.

This is the procedure you follow through all ten amendments of the Bill of Rights. As long as you can remember *just two words*—NAME RIGHTS—it will be hard for you *not* to remember all the cued sentences, once they are so filed. Try it and see for yourself.

On pages 86–87 is the complete Bill of Rights, all cued and connected to your mental file, NAME RIGHTS. Study the process carefully so that you understand exactly how to build and operate your own mental file cabinet to reliably store and retrieve any information you choose.

THE BILL OF RIGHTS

Mental File: N-A-M-E R-I-G-H-T-S

Mental File Cues	Information Units: Amendments 1 to 10	Cued Sentences to Memorize
N Engineers	Freedom of religion, speech, press, and right to assemble and petition.	Engineers make free religious speeches and assemble pressed partitions.
A Abe	Right to keep and bear arms.	Abe, the soldier, keeps his right to bear arms.
M Emma	Quartering of soldiers: Government is forbidden to quarter troops in a private home during wartime.	Emma, why can't we keep soldiers in our house during wartime?
E Eli	Freedom from unreasonable search and seizure.	Eli cannot search or seize your property.
R Artists	Trials for crimes, and just compensation: Grand jury indictment, no double jeopardy, no self-incrimination; due process and just compensation.	Artists jeopardize and incriminate themselves, but the grand jury justly compensates them in due process.
I Ike	Civil rights in trials: Speedy public trial, impartial jury, information regarding accusation, confrontation with witnesses, compulsory witnesses for the accused, and the right to counsel.	Ike was accused and confronted by witnesses, but he was informed he had the right to his own counsel and witnesses. He had a speedy public jury trial.
G Genial	Civil rights in civil suits: Trial by jury; facts tried by jury are not to be re-	Genial Ike said, "A civil jury trial suits me fine, but I don't want the final facts

Mental File Cues	Information Units: Amendments 1 to 10	Cued Sentences to Memorize
	examined.	to be <u>re-examined</u>.
H <u>H</u>-bombs	No excessive bail or fine, and no cruel and unusual punishment.	<u>H</u>-bombs bring <u>excessive bail</u>out and <u>fines</u>, because they are so <u>cruel and unusual</u>.
T <u>T</u>ea	Reserved rights of people: Constitutional rights cannot deny other rights.	<u>Tea</u> may not be a <u>constitutional right,</u> but you <u>cannot deny</u> me a cup!
S <u>S</u>pecial	Powers not constitutionally delegated to states are reserved to the states or the people.	<u>Special powers not stated</u> are <u>reserved</u> by the <u>people</u>. (In this last case, S is a <u>letter cue</u>. Just a reminder that these can be file cues when needed.)

This mental file, NAME RIGHTS, could just as easily have been RIGHT NAMES, AMEND RIGHT, or just one file word like REPUBLICAN, or CAMPGROUND, etc.

If you can't easily think up a word with the required number of different letters, just look in your dictionary. If you happen to think of a perfectly appropriate file word or phrase (and then you discover it has one repeated letter!), you can still use it *if* you don't use that repeated letter as a file cue (and you remember which one it is).

The main advantage of this unusual mental filing system is that the file word or phrase itself is so easy to remember. It is highly unlikely that you would forget these one or two simple words—*especially* since they have been the focal point of your concentration in creating and memorizing the complete mental file.

Once you have the cued sentences firmly in mind, just let each file cue trigger each sentence and you will be able to recall and reconstruct all the material so memorized. You have only to do this once to convince yourself.

HOW TO REVIEW YOUR MENTAL FILE

Once you have associated and memorized each file cue and its sentence, you have accomplished the first step. It's important for you to realize that even though you have memorized the material, it is still only in your temporary memory bank. It may last for hours or days, but if you want to *keep* this material ready for recall until exam time, you must continue to review from time to time.

Unlike other methods of memorizing which require books or notes for review purposes, all the material you mentally file is self-contained and responds to "built-in" reviewing. In other words, you can recall and review anything you have so memorized—anywhere, anytime. You merely call to mind your file cues and let them trigger back your cued sentences. Since you need no books or notes, you can review your mental files while you shower, do the dishes, shave, while you walk or ride to class, or during any other time that you don't usually use for study and review purposes. Do you see what this means? You can actually *increase* the time you have available for review—without decreasing the time you normally set aside for studying or other activities.

If you consider this carefully, you will realize that this attribute alone of mental filing is worth the small time and effort required to master it. Even by merely running through your mental files at the end of breakfast and lunch for a few days can effectively transfer this material to your long-term memory.

18

Variations in Mental Filing

THE SENTENCE FILE

The sentence file is a quick method of creating appropriate mental file cues. It is not necessarily *better* than the method you just learned, but when you're in a hurry and want to create a fast mental file, this will fill the bill.

Instead of using a single word (like REPUBLICAN) or a phrase (like NAME RIGHTS) as the basis of your mental file, you can use almost any appropriate *sentence* that you make up on the spot. Again, there are only two simple requirements:

1. The sentence file must have the same number of *words* as there are information units to memorize.
2. The first letter of each word should be different.

For example, as a sentence file for the Bill of Rights, we could use:

*T*he *B*ill *O*f *R*ights *L*ists *I*mportant *G*uarantees *F*or *E*very *C*itizen.

Instead of NAME RIGHTS, You simply remember the above sentence and use each of the first letters (T-B-O-R-L-I-G-F-E-C) in succession, as your file cues. If you can remember the easy sentence file, you will automatically know each file cue. This works the same as remembering the music staff. *"Every Good Boy Does Fine"* instantly gives you the name of the five lines, E-G-B-D-F. You may find it easier to come up with a quick sentence, rather than one word or phrase, because you can quickly "tailor make" any sentence to fit the subject matter you're about to file. Once you have your sentence file, you proceed as before.

THE ALPHABET FILE

The file systems you have learned so far are based on using alphabetical letters as file cues. But if you have more than 10 or 12 or so information units to memorize (the Bill of Rights had *ten*), you would need more file cues to handle them. The *Alphabet File* can handle *twenty-six* units of information to memorize, because the alphabet from A to Z has twenty-six letters—and you can use each of them, in succession, as file cues!

In this case, you don't have to think of a word, phrase, or sentence to create your mental file cues. With the alphabet, they are already made for you—and you know them by heart! So it's easy to think of them as file cues (they're *all* different), and you just mentally recall one after the other. It's no more difficult than reciting the alphabet.

For example, using the Bill of Rights again as our model, your first file cue would be *A,* and you might cue a few amendments this way:

Alphabet File Cue	Cued Sentence
A Apes	Apes give free religious speeches and assemble to press their petitions.
B Believe	Believe in your militia's right to keep and bear arms.
C See	See here! We don't have to keep soldiers in our house during a war.

The following are just a few similar-sound or letter cues that come to mine for each alphabetical letter. You may want to use this listing for reference.

Alphabet File Cue	Similar-Sound Cue or Letter Cue
A:	ape, Abe, aviator, Amos, ale, ate, aid, a, at, awful, atomic, ant.
B:	be, bee, before, between, beat, beam, beetle, beans, bleak, bat, bone.
C:	cease, cedar, ceded, ceiling, see, sea, seam, Cedric, coat, can.
D:	deed, deal, Dee, detail, detain, deliver, deep, drastic, doll, do.
E:	eel, eat, easy, eclair, Eli, epoxy, Easter, easel, every, earth.
F:	effort, Effie, effervesce, effect, fog, feet, fence, fabricate.
G:	Gee, Gene, genial, genius, Geology, geography, goat, gone, gooey.
H:	H-bomb, ancient, H, hole, hollow, horrible, high, happy, hoosier.
I:	I, Ike, ice, I'll, I'm Ira, isotope, icky, important, Indiana, ill.
J:	Jay, jaywalk, Jane, Jake, jade, Jail, Jupiter, Juno, jaguar, jog.

Alphabet File Cue	Similar-Sound Cue or Letter Cue
K:	Kay, Kate, kayo, keepsake, khaki, kickoff, kidnap, kidney, kinky.
L:	elevator, Elton, eldorado, Elsie, Ellen, like, liberty, loaf, loony.
M:	empire, Emma, emblem, embassy, motel, muff, maybe, Matterhorn, mate.
N:	engine, entire, enter, energy, nobody, nuts, nebula, never, nearly.
O:	Oh!, open, old, oboe, opal, opulent, opera, owl, out, objection.
P:	pea, Pete, piece, peel, peek, peep, Pluto, perfume, pretty, petal.
Q:	queue, cue, cute, cupid, quack, question, quintet, quorum, quibble.
R:	art, army, Arthur, are, arsenal, rabbit, rare, roar, radiator, read.
S:	eskimo, Esther, estimate, essay, soap, sorry, slick, scholarship.
T:	tea, tee, tease, team, teach, the, toad, toot, trapeze, total, them.
U:	Ukelele, uvula, ubiquitous, Uganda, you, Yukon, under, uncover, urgent.
V:	Venus, venal, vehicle, very, vibrate, verse, visual, vampire, voodoo.
W:	double you, double hue, wax, water, women, why, wonderful, wicked.
X:	except, extra, exhale, except, excellent, X-rated, X-ray, Xavier.
Y:	why, Wyoming, yacht, yesterday, year, yellow, yourself, young, Yule.
Z:	zebra, zenith, zero, zombie, zoo, zilch, zeppelin, zest, Zeus, zany.

THE NUMBER FILE

This kind of mental file works very much like the alphabet file. The only difference is that you use *numbers* for the file cues.

Most office filing systems have either an alphabetical or numerical file system, and there is no reason why you cannot operate these time tested and systematic methods within the province of your mind.

Here are a few number file cues plus similar-sound cues for each number. *Rhymes* are a specific type of similar-sound cue and work well with numbers.

Number File Cue	*Similar-Sound Cues*
ONE:	won, one, dun, ton, son, hun, pun, shun, run, done, gun, stun.
TWO:	to, too, two, shoe, glue, new, crew, strew, flew, blue, grew, blew.
THREE:	tree, free, three, be, bee, Bea, tea, sea, 3-D, me, lee, pea, she.
FOUR:	for, fore, four, score, gore, more, tore, lore, core, store, war.

With this number file, the first four amendments of the Bill of Rights might look something like this:

Number File Cue	*Cued Sentences*
ONE:	<u>One</u> has the <u>right</u> to make <u>free</u> <u>religious</u> <u>speeches</u> and <u>assemble</u> to <u>petition</u> the <u>press</u>.
TWO:	<u>To</u> <u>keep</u> and <u>bear</u> <u>arms</u> is the <u>right</u> of the <u>militia</u>.

(or)

<u>Lou</u>, the soldier, has the <u>right</u> to <u>keep</u> and <u>bear arms</u>.

Number
File
Cue   *Similar-Sound Cues*

THREE: Free thinkers won't keep soldiers in their houses
           during wartime.

FOUR: Fortunately, no one can search or seize your property.

Now here is the rest of the Number File through number twelve.

Number
File
Cue   *Similar-Sound Cues*

FIVE: hive, five, dive, Clive, live, chive, strive, drive.
SIX: bricks, licks, six, sticks, hicks, mix, fix, nix, tricks,
           kicks.
SEVEN: heaven, leaven, Kevin, Bevin, Evan, seven, seventh,
           Stephan.
EIGHT: ate, plate, eight, date, mate, Kate, late, gate, freight,
           bait.
NINE: wine, dine, fine, pine, nine, mine, sign, line, Rhine,
           brine.
TEN: hen, Ben, Len, den, ten, men, pen, when, Ken, tent,
           dent, went.
ELEVEN: leaven, eleven, elephant, Ella went, eleventh, heaven.
TWELVE: shelve, shelf, twelve, elf, elves, delve.

You may not want to use the Number File for more than 12 items; but if you do, turn back to the chapter on numbers for a more complete list of sound cues for numbers.

MENTAL FILING IN A NUTSHELL

You now have four mental files to use:

1. The Word or Phrase File
2. The Sentence File

3. The Alphabet File
4. The Number File

Each has its own merits and will accommodate any special materials you choose to memorize. The procedure is the same for the operation of each file:

1. Select the materials you wish to file.

2. Construct your initial Word, Phrase, or Sentence File. (The Alphabet and Number files are always ready. You don't have to "set them up" initially.)

3. Take the time to create your cued sentences.

4. Memorize each complete cued sentence. Go over each one until you know it perfectly. You will find that if your cued sentences are good ones, they will be surprisingly easy to remember after a few repetitions.

5. Periodically review your mental files. Simply call to mind each successive file cue, and let it trigger the rest of the material to mind. You can do your reviews at the end of meals, in the bathroom, or any other time that is convenient for you. This extra study time will in no way interfere with the other times you normally set aside for study. Don't forget that anything worthwhile takes some practice. If you find yourself thinking that creating and reviewing memory cues "takes too much time," resist such negative thoughts. Think instead of how much time and effort it takes to memorize difficult materials *without* a system to help you!

Mental filing will give you instant reviews of all filed information at any time or any place, without the specific need for books or notes. The file will hold all key points in the correct sequence, and any individual item can be located in the file merely by thinking of a specific file cue.

During exams, you are not normally allowed to consult your notes. But there is nothing to keep you from consulting your mental files! If you have effectively cued and reviewed your materials, they will spring to your mind almost as if you had your actual notes on your desk in front of you.

The Cue and Review File Systems you are now familiar

with can be used immediately. You don't have to "study and learn them first" to be able to apply them, as in standard mnemonic memory systems. Just apply them to your present memory needs and let them work for you. They will enable you to learn, retain, and reliably reconstruct and recall any information you choose.

PART IV:
MAKING IT STICK

19

Memory Reinforcement

You may be thinking, "How long will I be able to remember the things that I cue and review?" The answer is that you can remember this information for as long as you want to—for a day, a week, months, or years, depending on the following factors:

1. How well you learned the material in the first place.
2. How much you are willing to reinforce your impressions of that material.

With memory, as with so many other things, what you don't use, you will probably lose—to one degree or another. No one remembers everything; but to remember *anything,* the material must first be understood and then reviewed at intervals short enough so that what you are able to remember *can* be reviewed again. Of course, there are many things you do remember without reviewing at all—things that you may read, hear, or experience only once. For some reason, these things make such a deep impression that you remember them for years, if not a lifetime. For such things, you hardly need memory aids. But the vast majority of other things you study, learn, and wish to remember must be bolstered and reinforced by *use*—or they will probably be wiped clean by gradual memory fade-out.

Sometimes this fade-out may seem sudden rather than gradual. Have you ever noticed how much material you forget soon after an exam—especially one that involved plenty of cramming? The fact of the matter is that if you had continued (after the exam) to think about that material, or to use it occasionally in conversation, your recall of that material would be considerably better. As for remembering important information *until* the exam, the only genuinely reliable method to hold information in your head long enough to be tested on it is to keep reinforcing the impressions with periodic review.

CUEING AND REVIEWING

In all our cue and review exercises so far, the basic principle of review has been deliberately stressed. Cueing the material you wish to memorize makes it easier and quicker to *get* it memorized. But that's only the first step. In order to keep it accessible to recall, the reviewing is the magic ingredient. Each time you think about the material, recite it, use it, or mention it in conversation, you are hammering it more deeply into your long-term memory. Notice that I said even if you just *think about it,* the material is still being reinforced by repetition. It is meaningful repetition that strengthens the material in your mind so that you can remember it better, even with the passage of time. Your initial cueing and reviewing of material will accomplish temporary memorization more quickly and efficiently than any other method presently known. If your test is soon after your initial memorization (the same or next day, for example) you may not need more than one review session. But if your exam is weeks or months away, short periodic reviews of the information are necesary to keep it fresh in mind.

HOW TO SPACE YOUR REVIEWS

The act of learning something creates an actual change in your brain tissue. If this change is reinforced over a period of time, the changes can become permanent. Psychologists call this consolidation of the memory trace. It's important for you to know that the first consolidation takes place during the first ten minutes after initial learning. After this, further consolidation occurs during the day, while you sleep, and during the next few weeks. Most important, *consolidation takes place every time the same material is reviewed.* This is the reason for study, and for specific reviewing of your cued materials.

Scientific studies have shown that for most academic subjects and for most students, the most effective spacing for study and review is as follows:

1st review: within 5 to 10 minutes after the initial learning.

2nd review: later on during the same day.

3rd review: one week later.

4th review: one month later.

5th review: the same day as the exam, preferably just before.

Keep in mind that the spacing that is best for *you* may be greater or smaller. When you memorize materials with a mental filing method, it's a good idea to recall it and review it at the end of breakfast or lunch for a few days in succession. Let the end of a meal be your signal to look in your mental file. For general studying and reviewing you will hardly go wrong by following the above listed timetable for reviews. It makes the maximum use of your brain's natural consolidation, and ensures that your memory of the subject matter remains reliable and accessible.

If you find that certain subjects are more difficult (or boring), it is good common sense to double up on your reviews.

Remember that the initial process of cueing is creative and can spark increased interest, even in a dull subject—if you let it. If you can make your cues humorous in some way, all the better, but remember that effective cueing does not *have* to be funny or clever in order to work. What is important is that what *you* take the time to create, you will remember better. The act of creative cueing itself is actually concentration on the material in such a way that it already becomes almost half learned. As for humor, recent studies have shown that it can create a stronger initial memory impression; that's why many of the cues created during the writing of this book include a touch of humor.

RECITING AND REMEMBERING

Every time you recite your memorized cue sentences, you increase the strength of your memory for that material. You are actually rehearsing future retrieval of that material during the exam. The reason recitation is so effective is that by saying it, hearing it, thinking it, and feeling it (movement of your mouth and facial muscles), you are actually making a quadruple impression of the material on your brain. Psychologists call this multiple sensory registration and reinforcement. Remember that when you get all these things going for you at once—simple recitation combined with spaced reviews—you are giving your memory cells the kind of charge that will pay off at exam time.

THE ARC METHOD

This is an extra method of memory reinforcement that requires little if any effort on your part. It can be used any time, any place, and it will reinforce retention and recall of any kind of material—regardless of length. All you need for the ARC method is a cassette recorder. ARC is a letter cue for *A*utomatic *R*epetition by *C*assette.

Here is the method: Decide on the material you want to

memorize or review; then record it on a cassette. The material can be just your cued sentences, material from your notes, selections from your texts, or all the important material from all of your courses, if you so desire.

Suppose, for example, that you have four or five pages of text that you must know for a Tuesday morning test. Read the material onto your cassette, and then simply let the playbacks do all the repeating that you feel is necessary for you to grasp and retain the material. You listen, rewind, listen, rewind, and eventually such repetition can implant the material in your mind.

This does *not* mean that you have to sit for hours at a time, listening and rewinding. As with mental file reviews, you can listen to your cassettes at odd moments during the day or evening—when you are eating, doing the dishes, cleaning, bathing, walking, or just relaxing. The ARC method doesn't interfere with your regular study time at all.

Here's something interesting: Even if you don't give the playbacks your undivided attention, the continuous repetitions will eventually work their way into your mind and memory. Of course, if you *do* listen attentively, such reinforcement will be deeper and more lasting, and will happen faster.

Many professional speakers learn entire speeches this way. You can hardly escape the repetitions once the cassette is on, and even if you're not actually listening, the subliminal effect is working whether you are aware of it or not. Have you ever noticed how you remember phrases and sentences from commercials that you have seen repeatedly over a period of time? It's the same principle, and you can make it work for you, if you want to, with your cassette recorder.

Used intelligently, the ARC method can be a valuable and convenient means for extra memory reinforcement.

20

Memory and Examinations

How often have you had the feeling that you understood what you were reading, but wondered if you would remember it during the exam? All kinds of studies have shown that understanding the material does not at all guarantee that you will be able to remember it later. There are many reasons for this, including interference from other materials and situations, ineffective study habits, emotional stress, and other factors that may or may not be under your control.

One of the really basic reasons for inability to recall material, especially during exams, has to do with the phenomenon of "availability and accessibility." At Yale University, Endel Tulving's work showed that forgetting is not a problem of retention—but of retrieval. In other words, you do not necessarily "forget" at all. Rather, you experience *retrieval failure* because you can't seem to find the right retrieval cue to locate and release hidden information which, though still somewhere in your mind, remains inaccessible. It is available—but not accessible. It's like trying to locate a book in a large library. When you can't find it, this doesn't mean that the book isn't there. You may simply be looking on the wrong shelf or in the wrong section, or the book itself may be misplaced, making it inaccessible. Similarly, information you have studied is not really lost or forgotten, but it can be very difficult to recall to mind if you do not have the right retrieval cues.

A common example is when you can't think of the correct answer during an exam; but later, when you least need it, that information pops into your mind. Has a name or a fact ever been on the "tip of your tongue"—but for the life of you, you couldn't recall it? This is all clear evidence that such material is still in your memory, but that for some reason, it remains inaccessible.

The memory cue techniques you have learned in this book create specific retrieval cues that permit *direct access* to any material you so commit to memory. As you have experienced by now, these cues permit rapid memorization and rapid recall. This is because of the meaningful connections that were deliberately constructed for all the cued sentences. If you remember those connections, you remember the material. It is as simple as that.

With this in mind, it is important to remember that the best way to keep *any* study material accessible to recall is to review it periodically so that it can remain both available *and* accessible.

Nobody has to tell you that studying is work. But something you may have to be reminded of is that reading is not studying—it is reading. Your brain works primarily by association, organization, and reason. When you read difficult material and take the time to organize it, ask the right questions, and reason it out, the result is that the material makes sense and you are able to grasp its meaning. But "reading" didn't do it—*you* did.

A good question to keep in mind as you read is, "What are

the things I'm supposed to know?" Usually, most of your reading materials (and hopefully, your notes) are organized; things like chapter headings, introductions, italics, heavy print, and summaries are all good clues to the key facts, ideas, and concepts. These are the things you should consider for extra memory reinforcement.

21

Extra Memory Tips

GET RID OF DISTRACTIONS

If you are one of those people who can concentrate and study despite surrounding conversations, loud TV, barking dogs, and passing trains, this section is not for you. Most of us can't push a button in our minds and instantly tune out such distractions. It just doesn't work—and neither does your head—under such conditions. Granted, it's not always easy to eliminate such study interference, especially if you live in a dorm or house where noise and confusion is the norm. Unfortunately, the facts of life are still that in order to learn, you must study; and in order to study, you must do so under conditions that are favorable for effective studying. If you have a problem concerning noise, it must be solved before you can expect to achieve anything near your actual potential. It's up to you to create an atmosphere that will allow you decent and regular study.

DON'T STUDY WHEN YOU'RE TIRED

You can devote hours to a subject, but if you don't also give it *attention,* you're spinning your wheels as far as remembering is concerned. Everybody knows this, but you can still get caught in the trap of "tired study" without really being aware of it—until your head begins to nod. The only commonsense way to avoid this is to try to plan your study and review periods ahead, every day, and then to stick to them. Try to recognize in advance what activities will drain your energy, and then schedule your study time so that the two don't meet. Sometimes this is easier said than done; but being mentally alert and physically rested is so important that you should be reminded of this occasionally. The more alert you are during study, the more you will remember.

TAKE STUDY BREAKS

Wandering around gets you nowhere, and that goes for the mind as well. As soon as you notice that your mind wants to start wandering, it's time for a break. It's been known for years that short study periods are far more productive than one heroic study binge. You'll remember far more after three or four hour-long sessions—spaced out over four days—than you will after one eight-hour all-out effort.

EMPHASIZE UNDERSTANDING
INSTEAD OF PURE MEMORIZATION

Brute rote memorization of intricate materials can keep you up all night, and you can still blow it on the exam if you don't really understand what you've memorized. You can make things much easier for your memory if you look for *relationships* between facts, ideas, and concepts. Certain things, like some math formulas or equations or other abstractions may require rote memorization. When this happens, try to keep such repetitious memorization limited to short periods, say 20 or 30 minutes. Rote repetition becomes tiring, and you'll need a break to prevent mind wandering and fatigue.

For any memorizing, always try a cueing technique first, and you'll be working automatically with associative relationships for better understanding and longer lasting memory.

THE EFFECT OF TAKING NOTES ON MEMORY

Think of all your hours of study—trying to get all those facts into your head. Most people think that the head is the only seat of memory. But have you ever seen a person in his or her sixties get onto a bicycle for the first time in 30 years, and after a moment or two of uncertainty, begin to pedal, balance, and ride as well as he or she did 40 years ago? This happens because *muscle memory* remembers just as well (or better) than head memory.

The reason for this example is to make you aware that *taking notes* is muscle memory, and it will get you higher grades on an exam than just listening in class—even if you never study those notes at all.

If you feel that you can't listen well and take notes at the same time, try to write at least a few key points. Later you can rewrite them and fill in what you remember. All of this is thinking combined with muscle memory—which reinforces remembering all the more.

"MAKE NOISE"

It's easy to study or review passively and mechanically—with no particular attention or interest. But all you get for this kind of study is sleepy. Instead, get involved! Ask yourself questions, talk to yourself about the material, get up and pace the floor, write ideas as they occur to you. Recite your cues and recite them some more. With this kind of study and review, you will be hearing, seeing, touching, saying, and thinking the material—*plus* using your muscle memory. This multi-sensory input boosts your memory to an amazing degree. Studies show that *reciting* alone—even just once—increases the amount of material you remember from 25 to 100 percent.

CUE IT AND REVIEW IT

With the Cue and Review system, you've acquired a powerful new tool for memorizing and reliably recalling whatever material you choose. All you have to do now is to use it! Every time you do, you will have the confidence of control. This control will increase your motivation to learn, expand your confidence, and help you to relax when it's time for exams.

Bibliography

Atkinson, Richard C., and Shiffrin, Richard M. "The Control of Short-Term Memory," *Scientific American* (August 1971)

Baddeley, Allen D. *The Psychology of Memory*. New York: Basic Books, 1976

Bartlett, F. C. *Remembering*. Cambridge: University Press, 1932

Bower, Gordon H. "Analysis of a Mnemonic Device " *American Scientist* 58 (1970)

Bower, Gordon H., ed. *Human Memory*. New York: Academic Press, 1977

Bugelski, B. R. *Principles of Learning and Memory*. New York: Praeger Publishers, 1979

Herold, Mort. *You Can Have a Near-Perfect Memory*. Chicago: Contemporary Books, Inc. 1982

Herold, Mort. *A Memory System That Works*. Cassette-Workbook Course. Hazel Crest, Ill.: Memory Improvement Services, 1980

James, William. *Principles of Psychology,* Vol. 1. New York: Henry Holt & Co., 1890

Katona, George. *Organizing and Memorizing.* New York: Columbia University Press, 1940

Norman, Donald A. *Memory and Attention.* New York: John Wiley and Sons, 1976

Russell, Peter. *The Brain Book.* New York: Hawthorn, 1979

Sommer, Robert. *The Mind's Eye.* New York: Dell, 1978

Tulving, Endel. "Cue-Dependent Forgetting," *American Scientist* 62 (1974)

Yates, Frances A. *The Art of Memory.* Chicago: University of Chicago Press, 1966